Teaching Values:
An Idea Book
For Teachers
(And Parents)

Gary A. Davis

Westwood Publishing Company
Cross Plains, Wisconsin 53528

About the Author. Gary A. Davis is
Professor Emeritus of the University of
Wisconsin, Department of Educational
Psychology, in Madison, Wisconsin. He is
author of several college textbooks,
including *Creativity is Forever* (Kendall/
Hunt), *Education of the Gifted and Talented*
(with Sylvia Rimm; Allyn & Bacon), and
Handbook of Gifted Education (with Nicholas
Colangelo; Allyn & Bacon). In the values
area, *Values Are Forever* (also a Westwood
book) is an engaging 140-page workbook
for students in grades 4–8, or younger or
older. The author's interest in children's
values was born largely in listening to daily
teenage tragedies on station WBBM
Chicago. Many of these disasters might
have been prevented by helping children—
at a younger age—logically understand
values that are helpful versus hurtful,
productive versus self-destructive.

ISBN 1-888115-02-5

Library of Congress Catalog Card Number: 95-90783

How to Order:
Single or multiple copies may be ordered from Westwood Publishing Company, P. O. Box
222, Cross Plains, WI 53528. Telephone (608) 798-1040. Quantity discounts available. On
letterhead stationary, indicate intended use of the books (personal or classroom copy,
resale, library) and include purchase order number, check, money order, or credit card
type (VISA/MC) and number and expiration date.

Contents

Preface

Congratulations! Your interest in this book indicates that you share the author's concern with what's happening to many of today's kids. Perhaps that should be in a question form: What IS happening to many of today's kids? For the interest in teaching values has never been greater.

Some of us are old enough to compare today's parenting and teaching concerns with those of the 1940s, 1950s, and 1960s. Back then, parents worried about their kids cleaning up their rooms, taking a bath once in a while, being polite, using acceptable language, working hard in school, and not growing up to be a bum. In elementary school classes, teachers monitored values related to raising hands, taking turns, being quiet, respecting others' property, and not chewing gum or running down the hallways.

Sounds funny, doesn't it.

Today we worry about elementary children using or selling crack cocaine, joining gangs, carrying guns, getting shot, drinking booze, and in a couple of years contracting AIDS, getting pregnant, dropping out of school—and growing up to be a bum.

This book has a companion workbook filled with thought-provoking, awareness-raising, decision-forcing, and commitment-making exercises. *Values Are Forever* is a workbook for upper elementary and older children (grades 4–8, or younger or older). *Values Are Forever* focuses on the same purposes and same values as this book. Each of the books can stand on its own. Or *Values Are Forever* can be used to supplement, clarify, and embellish ideas related to the caring and constructive values that are the focus of this book.

A few of the word search and crossword puzzles in this book, along with three quizzes about values and rights and a more-or-less comical "Arithmetic Test" ("Subtracting the jerk, how many real friends do you have?"), were reproduced from *Values Are Forever*. However, most of the 11 word search and six crossword puzzles were created for this volume. The puzzles and quizzes were designed to be fun, as well as to stimulate children to think about values and make values decisions and commitments. Teachers are welcome to make copies for their *own* class (but please do not distribute them to every class in the district or sell them on the street).

As we will describe in Chapter 1, *Teaching Values* and *Values Are Forever* try to help kids understand values, the importance of values to their lives, and that poor values can be hurtful to others and destructive to themselves. Empathy is stressed throughout—"putting oneself in others' shoes"; imagining how others feel when they are hurt, treated rudely, stolen from, or otherwise treated badly; imagining how parents are hurt by their children's misbehavior or crimes; and imagining what others think about a child who pulls some thoughtless, rude, or hurtful stunt.

One recurrent theme might be called *futuristic* thinking. Children are encouraged to think about what their adult lives will be like if they adopt self-destructive values—such as dropping out of school, ignoring their health, joining a gang, or becoming an under-educated, under-trained person. And what their adult lives can be like if they adopt constructive, caring values, including valuing education and training. American suffering and poverty or the American Dream. Which is best? Which do you want? Then GO FOR IT!

Many of the values and exercises relate to teenage problems. It is important that children be prepared in advance for some of the values questions and difficulties they will face in middle and high school. *When they become teenagers, for many it is too late.*

Kids are the future and we love them a lot. This book is dedicated to helping some children, perhaps saving others. We want all children and youth to create better futures for themselves and become better citizens for all of society.

GAD

Children today love luxury too much. They have detestable manners, flout authority, have no respect for their elders. They no longer rise when their parents and teachers enter the room. What kind of awful creatures will they be when they grow up?

Socrates, 399 B. C.

We all make decisions that affect the course of our lives. . . . Your future is whatever you make it—so make it a good one!

Spoken by "Doc" in *Back to the Future, Part III*, by Steven Spielberg

Part I

Introduction

1

Dear Teacher (or Parent) . . .

The purpose of *Teaching Values: An Idea Book for Teachers (And Parents)* is to sketch some uncomplicated ideas for teaching values. The ultimate goal is to help children and youth understand what values are and discover why positive, constructive values are absolutely essential to their present and adult lives. Everyone benefits when young people learn constructive values.

A common recommendation for parents is to schedule "quality time" with their children. For parents and teachers, there may be no better use of "quality time" than helping children to think logically about values and to make commitments to positive values—values that are helpful, not hurtful, to others and themselves.

What Do the Activities and Exercises Try To Teach?

The approach is not subtle nor indirect. The strategies and exercises in *Teaching Values* were designed to help young people:

- Understand the meaning of "values" and their importance to our lives.
- Understand that our values determine who we are and what we will become.

- Understand that we have no right to mistreat others, and that others have no right to mistreat us.

- Understand that actions have consequences for others and ourselves.

- Think consciously, logically, critically, and creatively about healthy versus harmful values and behavior.

- Understand that we must make careful decisions and choices that will help—not hurt—ourselves and others.

- Empathize with people whose rights are violated by dishonesty, vandalism, or rude and hurtful behavior—the victims.

- Discover why some values are desirable and others are hurtful by weighing the consequences of bad attitudes and behavior versus positive attitudes and behavior.

- Understand that we will respect ourselves and others will respect us if we embrace constructive values.

- Value education, achievement, and career preparation.

- Make strong personal commitments to constructive values and behavior.

- Become "inoculated" against media content and peer pressures that promote, for example, dishonesty, rudeness, bad manners, under-achievement, dropping out, violence, crime, drug use, and lack of concern for others' rights and the environment.

Four concepts in the above list are critical. The first is **LOGICAL DISCOVERY,** perhaps self-discovery of ethical principles. Lecturing at kids to "be good" doesn't work for everyone. (Some would argue that "lecturing at" doesn't work for anyone!) The approach in this idea book is to guide children to *discover for themselves* why some values and behavior are good for others and themselves, and why other values and behavior are hurtful to others and themselves.

EMPATHY is a second key feature. If children learn to "put themselves in others' shoes" and imagine others' feelings or the consequences to others of bad behavior, they will be less likely to treat others rudely or unfairly or to hurt them physically or psychologically. (Yes, empathy lies at the core of the Golden Rule of Christianity and comparable guideposts in other world religions.) As an example, consider one of the worst, yet common, values among America's gang members. Hating and killing members of rival gangs is valued; revenge is deemed essential. Gang members talk about killing so lightly that murder has nicknames: "Snuff," "blow away," "pop," and simply "do." Do these violent young people stop and think, "Gee, I would not want to be shot," "I would not want to be killed," "I have a life to live"? Do they think about the feelings of the mothers, fathers, or other relatives and friends of their victims? It seems that the accepted value and the depth of thoughtful concern are reflected in "So long sucker!" Valuing the killing of rival gang members and others who offend (e.g., in traffic), along with a seemingly total lack of empathy, probably underlies much of today's record-setting murder rates by young people.

Third, **PERSONAL COMMITMENT** to good values is essential. Understanding *reasons* for good values (through logical discovery) and understanding others' *feelings* (empathy) are necessary. But an indispensable step is getting kids to consciously acknowledge "Yes, this value is good for others and for me, I will try hard to do this" and "No, that value is hurtful to others and to me, I should not do that"

Fourth, **RESPECTING OTHERS' RIGHTS** to fair and cordial treatment runs throughout all principles and activities in this book. Respecting others' rights relates closely to the ability to have empathy: If one understands others' feelings, one is less likely to violate their rights.

In sum, the strategies and activities in this book were created to help children and youth comprehend what values are, how values guide behavior, and how productive values can help them reach more satisfying and productive lives. The activities help them grasp how poor values can make life difficult—or as we see in daily big-city news reports, how poor values can trash their lives *permanently*! Empathy and raised awareness of our rights and others' rights are central.

About Teaching Values

There always has been a need to teach values that are positive, constructive, and healthy. As a general trend, parents, educators, and religious instructors are, in fact, succeeding. The vast majority of children and youth—who do NOT make the daily crime reports—understand early on that responsibility, honesty, fair-mindedness, pleasantness, and respect for others' rights is logically and sensibly the best way to live. They understand that getting an education or technical training will help them reach satisfying and productive adult lives. They come to value the respect and dignity that comes with ethical behavior.

So much for the good news. We also know too well that today the need to help children and youth embrace basic virtues is DESPERATE. The daily news in big cities, and weekly news in medium cities, describe "drive by" killings, drug use and dealing, tossing newborn babies into dumpsters, rape, and other criminal and violent behavior—the majority of which is committed by young people. Even elementary children are persuaded to take drugs and join gangs. Some bring guns to school—"For protection," "To feel powerful," or "To show my friends." The following are some sample recent news items: (1) A 13-year-old Racine, Wisconsin, boy shot and killed a 14-year-old because the latter flashed a gang sign. (2) A 16-year-old Milwaukee girl was robbed and then raped at gun point for three-hours (2:00 a.m. until dawn) by three teenagers; *the leader was 11 years old*. (3) In Wausau, Wisconsin, a city of just 32,000, word spread that gang members planned to randomly shoot into a crowd during a Fourth of July fireworks display. The threat was believed, and fireworks plans were altered. (4) In Salt Lake City two rival gang members in a store parking lot shot each other at close range, falling dead on top of each other. (5) In Chicago an 11-year-old boy accidentally killed a 14-year-old girl while shooting at someone else. His pals executed him for attracting attention to their gang. (6) A woman driver cut in front of a carload of young males, who opened fire, killing the woman's young daughter.

Lesser violations of others' rights and self-destructive behaviors—rudeness, disruptiveness, petty theft, vandalism, wastefulness, making messes for others to clean up (including the ever-popular pitching of burger wrappers and beer cans out the car window), and dropping out of school—do not make the news, but clearly need attention. One assistant high school principal earned himself a spot on national news by suspending 100 of his 700 students—"until they agree to behave themselves." The remaining 600 students applauded his seemingly outrageous gesture.

Regrettably, some parents, who perhaps are uneducated and struggling to survive, do not or cannot serve as role models for good citizenship and valuing education. In extreme cases, children LEARN disastrous values from parents and other family members. Imagine a family in which mom is on cocaine and welfare, dad is in prison, older siblings are thieves and drug dealers, everybody is short-tempered and violent, and nobody stayed in school.

In some minority groups, children who study hard or even stay in school are reproached by peers for "acting white"—an attitude that is at once self-destructive yet commonplace. At a recent conference on gifted education, your author was told of a brilliant African American high school youth with great academic talent and marvelous leadership gifts. He was smart enough to weigh the choice between peer acceptance—which meant joining a gang—versus being a scholar and an eventual professional person. He chose the gang, stopped studying, began failing classes, and then dropped out of high school entirely. A personal tragedy, a loss to society.

Should Values Be Taught In School?

There are some—fewer all the time—who believe that values should *not* be taught in school. Values, they argue, are the province of the home and the church. Two points seem relevant. First, the level of moral thinking among many of today's youth suggests that some homes and churches (and schools) are failing with flying colors. Second, values always have been taught in school and they always will be. Values relating to friendliness, courtesy, patriotism, honesty, fairness, hygiene and health, and appreciation for the sciences, the arts, one's culture, and education itself have long been legitimate substance for values education in the classroom. "Teaching values" is camouflaged under the acceptable label "Citizenship."

Consider this statement copied from a kindergarten poster in Rochester, New York:

> We, the kindergartners in room 14, have decided that in order to be able to learn, we must:
>
> 1. Keep our hands and feet to ourselves.
>
> 2. Use soft voices and nice language.
>
> 3. Be good listeners and don't interrupt.
>
> 4. Be kind to one another.

Wouldn't it be wonderful if the kindergartners in room 14, and kindergartners everywhere, could carry these messages with them into the upper grades, middle school, high school, and adult life?

Your Values? My Values? Universal Values?

Another issue which some consider sticky is "Who's values do we teach, yours or mine?" Some values are *universal*—they are good for everyone and should be adopted by everyone. The reader no doubt can think of grey areas and value conflicts ("Do I steal for my hungry children?" "Do I rat on my friend?" "Should I break the law and speed my wife to the delivery room?" "Should cancer be treated with marijuana?"). The essential criterion of universal values is:

Does the behavior hurt others or ourselves?

If it does, we probably would agree that it is wrong, and children and youth should learn **not** to do it.

Consider whether the following values might be considered universal; that is, noncontroversial, good for everyone and society:

Honesty

Trustworthiness

Responsibility

Respect for the rights and property of others

Understanding the problems, feelings, and viewpoints of others

A sense of democracy and fair play

Cleanliness, neatness

Pleasantness, good manners

Getting along with others

Cooperation, helpfulness

Self-understanding, self-respect, self-esteem, confidence

Respect from others

Good health

Conservation mindedness

An education and achievement orientation

A sense of control over one's destiny

Respecting the elderly, handicapped, and others who are different

This book tries to avoid controversial values—ones about which thoughtful people can disagree (e.g., hunting animals, abortion, school prayer).

Why This Book?

A loudly proclaimed solution to today's high crime rate is "Build more prisons!" While probably necessary, a better long-term solution is to start with children—like the kindergartners in room 14. We *must* help them understand why honest and fair behavior is better for them personally and for everyone else, and why education and training are essential to their own future. We must help them take control of their lives and make deep commitments to positive and productive behavior.

In the area of gifted education, a frequently cited truism is that "Tomorrow's leaders are in today's schools." It is equally true that tomorrow's thieves, murderers, rapists, wife beaters, litterers, drug dealers, drunks, unskilled, unemployed, unpleasant, unfair, rude, cruel, irresponsible, and unhappy adults also are in today's schools. Too many will be in tomorrow's prisons. Or tomorrow's cemeteries.

2

Two Theories of Moral Development

(In Less Than Six Pages)

If you have taking a college course in human development or general educational psychology, you might be acquainted with two theories of moral development: Benjamin Bloom's *Taxonomy of Educational Objectives: Affective Domain* (Krathwohl, Bloom, & Masia, 1964) and Lawrence Kohlberg's (1976) stages of moral development.

Taxonomy Of Affective Objectives

Bloom's "affective taxonomy" was proposed as a description of learning values and attitudes, and therefore as a guide for teaching values and attitudes. It is comprised of five main levels:

Level 1. Receiving

At this level a teacher or parent wants children to become aware of a values concern (such as compassion, education, drug use, or criminality) and willing to receive more information about it.

Level 2. Responding

In Level 2 children first simply accept the adult's attitudes (acquiescence), and then become willing to actively explore the problem and possible solutions.

Level 3. Valuing

Here, the value becomes progressively more accepted as genuine and personal. Children's behavior becomes consistent with the value. They may even feel committed to taking action.

Level 4. Organization

At Level 4 a value becomes integrated with other values. For example, the value of *compassion* becomes integrated with values relating to education, society, government, money, life goals, and so on.

Level 5. Characterization by a value complex

In this final step the particular value (or attitude) becomes a permanent part of the person's value system and life philosophy. A person sees himself or herself as honest, compassionate, concerned for the environment, and so forth. Someone in this stage might seek a career related to a particular set of values. For example, a compassionate person might wish to become a social worker or nurse.

Kohlberg's Stages In Moral Development

Harvard psychologist Lawrence Kohlberg studied the same group of 75 boys over a period of twelve years. Based upon their changing moral reasoning, he developed a model of moral thinking that helps us understand the sequence of stages through which moral thinking proceeds. He also outlined implications of the model for teaching values and moral thinking.

Kohlberg's stages are said to be "true, invariant stages," which means:

- They occur one at a time.
- They always occur in the same order.

- Movement is always forward, never backward.
- A person may be in only one stage at a time.
- Every person proceeds through the stages in the same order.
- Stages are never skipped.
- Importantly, growth may stop at any stage and at any age.

Kohlberg's stages of moral development are divided into three levels, the *Preconventional*, *Conventional*, and *Postconventional* levels, each of which includes two substages.

Preconventional Level

Both stages of the *Preconventional* level evolve around the physical consequences of an action—regardless of any ethical meaning or value the action may have.

Stage 1. The child is oriented toward rewards and punishments. There is complete deference to authority and physical power. *Why obey rules? To avoid punishment.*

Stage 2. Right action is that which satisfies one's own needs and sometimes the needs of others—who will reciprocate. Concepts of "fairness" and "equal sharing" are based purely on practical considerations, not high-level principles of justice. *Why obey rules? To obtain rewards or have favors returned.*

Conventional Level

The *Conventional* level also includes conformity, but now "good" and "bad" are defined by the expectations and rules of others—the person's family, community, or nation. "Good behavior" is that which pleases and is approved by others, or is dictated by authority or law. Many people—children and adults—never progress beyond Conventional level morality.

Stage 3. "Good behavior" and "being nice" are desirable because they please others. In this "good boy/good girl" stage there is much conformity to stereotypes. *Why obey rules? To avoid disapproval or dislike.*

Stage 4. Stage 4 includes deference to rules and authority and the maintenance—not revision—of the social system. "Good behavior" means respecting the law and doing what authority figures say is correct. The person may realize that laws and rules exist to preserve the social order. Respect is earned through dutiful conformity. *Why obey rules? To avoid censure from legitimate authority (and avoid the resulting guilt).*

Postconventional Level

Now the good stuff. The *Postconventional* level includes universal and personal moral principles that are valid apart from authority. For example, the Golden Rule ("Do unto others . . .") represents postconventional thinking. It is highly desirable to think at this level.

Stage 5. Right action is defined by rights, standards, rules, and laws that have been examined and agreed on by society. However, consideration of individual rights and values (equality, fair play) leave open the possibility of rationally changing the standards, not freezing them as in Stage 4. Stage 5 is said to represent the "official morality" of American government. *Why obey rules? To maintain community welfare and gain the respect of others.*

Stage 6. Finally, for the select few, the highest stage of moral development is an orientation toward decisions of personal conscience and self-chosen ethics, based upon consistent universal principles and rights. Some examples are justice, equality of human rights, respect for individual differences, dignity, and the Golden Rule.

Kohlberg found that children and adolescents understand all stages up to their own—and only one additional stage. Significantly, they prefer this next higher stage. A child often moves to the next higher stage when he or she is confronted with the attractive views of a peer (or parent, or teacher) who is thinking at this next higher stage.

As for teaching moral thinking:

1. Kohlberg is best known for recommending that children practice discussing and making decisions in moral issues that require a higher level of moral thinking. He also recommends exposing children to concepts one step higher than their current stage, and encouraging them to think at this more mature stage.

2. Kohlberg further suggested having children role play someone who has, for example, been cheated, treated rudely, abused by an authority, or who must put their suffering pet to sleep.

For middle and high school students, or perhaps mature younger children, *the three levels (and perhaps the specific six stages)* can be good curriculum content. Discussing these can stimulate an understanding of values and moral thinking and foster commitment to higher stages of values and ethics.

The three main stages can be simplified quite handily. For example:

In *Preconventional* thinking, people only worry about rewards and punishments. They think, "It's OK to steal somebody's bicycle or dog if I don't get caught"; or "It's OK to kill somebody if I don't get caught"; or "I'll be nice to grandmother, but only because she might give me a dollar." Is this a good way to think? Why not? Discussions might include teenagers who steal or even murder because they believe it will be good for themselves—without thinking of the rights, feelings, or lives of others.

In *Conventional* thinking people just do what others say they should—"I'd better follow the rules, be pleasant, and use good manners or else people will think I'm a jerk"; "I can't park here because it's against the law." Discussion can focus on the difference between rigid "law'n order" and "rules are rules" thinking, versus behaving fairly and nicely because it's the right thing to do (Postconventional thinking).

In Postconventional thinking, intelligent people choose their own good values and ethics based upon fairness and respecting others' rights—"I will not hurt others because it is simply not right; I would not want others to hurt me."

Moral Development Theory And This Book

Regarding Bloom's taxonomic steps in the development of a value or attitude, the exercises and activities in this book were not deliberately created with the five steps in mind. However, virtually all activities do, in fact, begin by raising awareness of a values problem; then elicit responses related to the value; then help children understand and accept the value; and finally, encourage children to make a commitment to the value.

The implications of Kohlberg's stages, especially the three main levels, should be obvious. The goal throughout the present activities and exercises is to stimulate thinking at higher moral levels. Especially, a teacher or parent should be aware of, and draw children's attention to, examples of moral thinking that are guided only by rewards and punishments (Preconventional thinking) or by blind conformity to peer traditions or unreasonable rules (Conventional thinking).

With elementary children, we want to move them—at the very least— from Preconventional behavior guided only by selfish concerns for personal benefit ("Cheating and stealing are great, just don't get caught!") into more beneficial Conventional thinking. The ideal goal, of course, is Postconventional thinking based, in its simplest form, on the effects of good or bad behavior upon others or ourselves.

References

Kohlberg, L. (1976). Moral states and moralization: The cognitive developmental approach. In T. Lickona (Ed.), *Moral development and behavior*. New York: Holt.

Krathwohl, D., Bloom, B. S., & Masia, B. (1964). *Taxonomy of educational objectives. Handbook II: Affective domain*. New York: McKay.

3

A Word About Decisions and Choices

A theme that can run throughout your guidance of children's values is that of decisions and choices.[1] As parent or teacher, you can raise children's awareness that every day they make decisions and choices. Some Decisions are little decisions. Little decisions do not affect our lives very much. These are examples of little decisions:

Should I eat *Cheerios* or *Mini-Wheats* for breakfast?

Which shirt will I wear to school today?

Should I tie my shoes or let them flop open?

Should I take my yellow pencil or my green pencil?

Should I have a hot dog or a slice of pizza for lunch today?

Should I rest on my left elbow or my right elbow?

Should I buy the red gym shorts or the blue ones?

Should I eat some *Peanut M & M*s or plain *M & M*s.

Grownups make little decisions, too:

Should I buy the blouse with the long sleeves or the short sleeves?

Should we have spaghetti for dinner, or maybe chicken soup?

[1]Parts of this Chapter are adapted from *Values Are Forever.*

Should I go shopping tonight, or wait until tomorrow?

Little Decisions will NOT affect:

Who you are.

How you see yourself.

What people think of you (at least not much).

Your chances for a good future life.

What you will become.

Other decisions are BIG DECISIONS. They are BIG DECISIONS because they affect your life, maybe a lot, maybe even ruin it. Permanently. These are some BIG DECISIONS:

Should I be dishonest? Should I steal things from people's desks, lockers, or coat pockets every chance I get?

Should I steal things from the department store, drug store, toy store, and record store?

Should I tell lots of lies, break promises, and borrow things and never return them?

Or should I be an honest person? Should I be trustworthy? Should I be someone whom others respect? Someone whom I can respect?

Should I be a bully? Should I push people around, especially the little kids?

Or should I think about what it's like to be bullied and pushed around, and not do it?

Should I be rude and loud? Should I yell at people? Shoot my mouth off in class? Put people down every chance I get? ("Don't be so dumb, Jackie!" "What an ugly shirt, Chris!")

Should I have a bad temper and be grouchy? Should I snap at my parents, my friends, and even my teacher whenever I feel like it?

Should I play my boom box real loud—and make everybody listen to my music, whether they like it or not?

Or should I respect other people's right to honest and pleasant treatment? Should I be pleasant and helpful? Should I give compliments? ("Good idea, Jackie!" "Nice shirt, Chris!")

Should I be lazy in school, try to avoid work, and try not to learn anything?

Should I plan right now to drop out of school as soon as I can?

Or should I try hard to learn, so I will understand my world? And so I can get a good job after high school, or go on to a technical school or college?

Should I ignore my health? Should I eat lots of junk? Not get any exercise (except pushing TV buttons)? Start smoking right away?

Or should I take care of my body, eat well, get exercise, maybe even get on soccer and softball teams? And live healthier and probably longer.

Of course, you stress that BIG DECISIONS are the important ones. BIG DECISIONS affect:

WHO WE ARE. We can enjoy who we are and respect ourselves. Or we can end up wishing we would have made better decisions.

HOW WE SEE OURSELVES. We can be proud of ourselves and what we do with our lives. Or we can end up wishing we would have been more careful with our lives.

HOW OTHERS SEE US. If we decide to be pleasant people, honest people, people who are willing to work for what we want, others will respect us. If we make bad decisions—and become unpleasant, dishonest, and uneducated—we lose respect.

WHAT WE WILL BECOME. If we make good decisions, we have a much better chance for a successful, enjoyable, and easier Life.

Perhaps critically, parents and teachers should stress that A LOT of middle school and high school students make BIG DECISIONS that hurt themselves badly. For example:

Some teenagers decide to be unpleasant, grouchy, nasty, messy people that nobody likes (except other unpleasant, grouchy, nasty, messy people).

Many decide to drop out of school—and then are unhappy because they need money, but can't get a good job.

Some ruin their health. They take drugs, drink a lot of booze, smoke a pack of cigarettes a day, and maybe catch some diseases.

Many teenagers get drunk, drive cars and motorcycles wildly—and kill themselves and/or others.

Some decide to bring guns to school because they think it's cool and it makes them feel "tough" and "powerful." They risk shooting someone.

Some decide to rob Stop-and-Go (7-11) stores—and are sent to juvenile detention centers or state prisons.

Some decide to sell drugs because they think they will get rich. They end up in prison too, if they don't get killed by the kids who carry guns.

Some teenagers decide to join gangs. The gang members tell each other that it's cool to bring a gun to school, drop out of school, become criminals, terrorize everybody in the neighborhood, take drugs, and sell drugs. Sometimes they shoot members of other gangs. (Over half of all gang members end up in prison or dead before they are 25 years old!)

Some high school students don't even THINK about getting job skills or professional training. After high school, they have BIG trouble finding a good job or career.

Other middle-school and high-school students make better "BIG DECISIONS."

They want to respect themselves.

They want others to respect them.

They want to make a good life for themselves and their future families.

They try not to mess up their lives.

They don't do the things in the previous list.

You can slip in some "What would happen if . . . ?" or "Which is best . . . ?" questions if it helps drive a point home.

What would happen if you dropped out of high school?

What would happen if you had a gun, got sore, and shot somebody?

What would happen if you decided to be a rude, unpleasant jerk?

Which is best, to have professional training and earn good money at a job you like? Or have no training and find only minimum wage jobs?

Which is best, to spend your life with a loving partner, perhaps have children? Or to make ONE BAD DECISION and live most of your life in a cage (prison).

Which is best, to have people like you and respect you? Or to think you are a rude, unpleasant person.

Which is best, to be an honest, trustworthy person with self-respect and respect from others. Or someone who lies, steals, cheats, breaks promises, and borrows things and never returns them—someone people cannot trust.

Using News Reports

Decisions and choices. It's relatively easy to find instructive examples of teenagers (especially) who make bad decisions and choices and cause immense problems for themselves. With ONE thoughtless bad decision they trash their lives. News stories, usually from medium-to-large cities, provide an endless supply of teenage tragedies that a parent or teacher can use to help children logically understand and embrace values that can protect them. Too many teenage mistakes are in the "BIG DECISIONS" categories noted above. For example, many teenagers ruin their lives with fatal drunk driving accidents (especially on graduation night), drug use, drug dealing, car thefts, robberies, beatings, shootings, "car jacking," AIDS, abusing unwanted babies or discarding them in trash cans, and so on. These happen daily. They harm or destroy lives, dreams, and aspirations.

Some sample dialogues might sound something like the following:

1. "Did you hear about Rafael Johansen at Central High? He got blotto drunk on graduation night and was killed in a car wreck. Killed his girl friend, too."

   Could this kind of mistake happen to anyone? Could it happen to you? (You bet it could!)

   When you are dead, is that temporary or permanent?

   Will Rafael get another chance to do it right, to not drink so much? Why not?

   Does this mean you have to be careful NOT to make even ONE big deadly mistake?

Kids get a little wild on graduation night, don't they.

But do you think it is a good idea NOT to kill yourself?

What do you suppose the problem was? (Drinking; drinking too much; not being experienced with booze; not being able to tell how drunk he was.)

Do you think this horrible accident could have been avoided? How?

Are you the type of dummy who would get drunk, drive out of control, and kill yourself and maybe a few of your friends?

2. "Hmmm. Some gang members got drunk and did a drive-by shooting that killed a little girl. They're all going to prison for 20 years."

Is this a horrible tragedy?

How do you suppose the little girl's family feels?

How do you think the boys will like it in prison for 20 years?

Do you think they would rather do something else with their lives?

How do you think the boys' families feel about all of this? Are they happy? Sad?

Did the boys make a HUGE mistake? A huge BAD DECISION?

Why didn't they think about what they were doing?

Early Training in Decision Making and Responsibility[2]

Parents can help develop responsible thinking in young children—including good decision making and problem solving—by giving them opportunities to make choices and decisions, to be trusted and depended upon. Most parents are in the habit of making all decisions for children (it's easier and faster); some revising of those habits may be necessary.

To help young children begin *making responsible decisions*, let them choose, for example, whether to wear their old sneakers or the new ones to the shopping mall; whether they want orange juice or Cranapple juice with a snack. Let them select which toy they would like to play with first, which

[2]Some ideas for this section were drawn from S. G. Cooper, "Decision Making: Meeting the Needs of Educators and Parents," Delta Kappa Gamma Bulletin, 1995, 61(2), 35–38.

book or cassette they would like to hear. In a word, let them make choices and decisions whenever possible.

Also let them *think of options and alternatives*, for example, "What are some things you/we could do this morning? Give me a bunch of ideas."

When possible, let children *solve problems* and *"figure things out"* on their own. It helps develop thinking skills, independent thinking, and responsibility—even though it always is tempting for the parent to say, "Here, let me do it for you."

As children grow older, the complexity of their decision making and problem solving also can grow. For example, when children have money (from allowances, chores, or birthday gifts) let them *decide* how to spend it. In addition to practice making decisions, they also will learn that "When it's gone, it's gone."

Of course, parents monitor their children's decision making and problem solving. At times a parent may need to suggest acceptable alternatives. "No, we don't eat *Cracker Jacks* for breakfast. How about *Cheerios, Crispy Critters, Cap'n Crunch,* or *Mini-Wheats*?"

Also, when necessary, a parent can help children consider the consequences of questionable choices. "I dunno Pat, if you spend all your birthday money on that tent, you won't have any left for the soccer ball or gym bag you've been talking about. What do you think you ought to do?"

Some benefits of strengthening children's decision-making and problem solving are these:

- Children develop responsibility, maturity, and independent thinking.
- They learn to make good decisions on their own, whether or not an adult is present.
- They come to feel more competent; they develop feelings of "I can."
- They learn that they have control over their lives—which is the most important factor affecting school success and high career aspirations.
- Their self-esteem improves.
- Independence, rather than conformity, is fostered.
- Good judgment and independence help them "see though" messages of violence and other negative values portrayed on television.

■ They may make better decisions and judgments relating to friends, family, social activities, school work, sports, jobs, and other important areas.

As a final thought for this chapter on decisions and choices, let's ponder again Doc's words in *Back to the Future III*:

We all make decisions that affect the course of our lives. . . . Your future is whatever you make it—so make it a good one!

Part II

Overview of Strategies and Activities

Chapter

4

Strategies and Activities

The following chapter, Chapter 5, will emphasize what teachers and most parents already know—that children learn values from teachers, parents, older siblings, other neighborhood and school children, and TV and movies. Chapter 5 will elaborate on how to capitalize on the most common, yet most powerful, home and classroom mechanism for teaching constructive values—*modeling* good values in what you say and do.

In addition to good models, children also benefit from what educators and psychologists call *metacognition*. Metacognition means "thinking about thinking." In a values context, metacognition means "thinking about one's own values." Children need become aware (1) of what values are, (2) that values guide their decisions and behavior, and (3) that good and bad values will affect their entire lives in good and bad ways. Children also can learn where their values come from (home, school, church, peers, TV/movies). Saturday cartoons and most movies teach both positive, constructive values and negative, destructive ones. When children stay up for later TV programs, shows such as *MTV* and *Beavis and Butt Head* send unsubtle damaging messages about values. An effort should be made to *inoculate* children against potentially harmful messages. We will return to modeling and how to try to offset TV and movie damage to values in Chapter 5.

What and How

Aside from modeling and seeking to offset peer and TV influence, let's look at *what* the exercises and activities in this book seek to teach, and *how* the values are taught.

You may have noticed from the table of contents that the main body of this book is organized around values categories. For example, Part III is Honesty and Trustworthiness, Part IV is Rights of Others, and so on. Within each values category, chapters are organized according to types of learning activities: "What would happen if . . . ?", brainstorming, visualization, and others. Very often, the exercises in specific chapters spill over into more than one value category. For example, a brainstorming activity about "honesty" implicitly covers "rights of others" as well.

The types of attitudes and values that can be the focus of home and classroom exercises and discussions are summarized in Table 4.1. All are intended to be noncontroversial, universal values—good for everyone, good for society. Perhaps you can add to the list.

As we noted in Chapter 1, the parent and teacher activities—including your modeling of good values and the discussions, activities, and exercises described in this book—are intended to help children:

■ Become more aware of their values and attitudes.

■ Understand that values determine their identities—who they are—and their adult lives.

■ Empathize with victims of bad behavior.

■ Make strong commitments to positive attitudes, values, and behavior.

> The strategies should help children decide, "Yes, I am an honest, caring person," and "Yes, I want to be a trained, capable adult."

Most activities and exercises in this book require creative thinking and imagination. The specific main strategies are:

■ Taking a Problem Solving Approach (Chapter 5 only)

■ "What Would Happen If . . . ?"

- Brainstorming
- Reverse Brainstorming
- Analogical Thinking
- Taking Other People's Perspectives
- Visualization
- Questioning and Discussion

Throughout the exercises, children creatively generate ideas, think of logical reasons, visualize, think analogically, take other perspectives (empathize), and think logically, reasonably, critically, and evaluatively about helpful and hurtful behavior.

Table 4.1. Summary of Categories and Specific Values

I. HONESTY, TRUSTWORTHINESS

Not Cheating	Returning Things
Not Stealing/Shop Lifting	Keeping Promises
Not Lying	Not Vandalizing

II. RIGHTS OF OTHERS

Rights of Other Children, Teachers, Family, Friends	Not Bullying, Teasing, Criticizing, Calling Names
Rights of the Elderly, Disabled, Others in the Community	Not Hurting Others
Accepting Individual Differences	Empathizing With Others' Problems
Friendliness, Helping Others	Respect for Others' Property

III. PERSONAL DEVELOPMENT

Accepting Responsibility	Valuing Friends, Treating Friends Well
Accepting Consequences	
Valuing Health, Hygiene	Respect, Self-Respect, Pride
Caring, Compassion	Developing One's Talents
Controlling One' Temper	Sense of Fair Play, Democracy
Caring For Animals	

(continued)

Table 4.1, Continued

IV. MANNERS

Asking	Being Courteous and
Waiting, Patience	Pleasant (Not Rude)
Sharing	Being Considerate with
Behaving Properly in Public	Elderly, Handicapped,
Doing Favors	Persons who are "Different"

V. SCHOOL AND WORK HABITS

Paying Attention	Valuing Education
Promptness	Achievement Motivation,
Perseverance, Doing a	Self-Motivation
Good Job	Understanding Purposes of
Using Time Wisely	Rules
Observing Safety Rules	Accepting Leadership,
Doing Neat Work	Followership Roles

VI. ENERGY AND ENVIRONMENT

Conserving Heat, Electricity	Caring for own Property
Conserving Natural Resources	Caring for Others' Property
Conserving School Materials	Not Being a Messy Person
Not Littering	

In addition to the techniques in the above list, other exercises may be copied for use in the classroom (or home). These include (1) word search and crossword puzzles, which raise awareness of values words and concepts, (2) values quizzes, which stimulate children to think about and make decisions about values, and (3) one "arithmetic test." ("You have four friends. One is a liar, a cheat, and a thief and steals your cassettes. How many *good* friends do you have?")

Create-Them-Yourself Values Exercises

One benefit of the main strategies in this book is that they are simple. You can modify them to create original exercises to fit the moral thinking needs of particular children of any age or background. Some young people need to stop wasting paper, disturbing others, or sailing airplanes or to think more about college or technical training. Others need to grasp the hurtful and self-destructive consequences of terrorizing younger children, stealing, vandalizing, taking drugs, joining gangs, carrying guns, gambling on AIDS, and dropping out of school.

What Would Happen If . . . ?"

"What would happen if . . . ?" is a traditional creative thinking strategy that is used to stimulate imagination ("What would happen if we had an eye in the back of our head?") and encourage futuristic thinking (e.g., "What would happen if the world ran out of oil?"). "What would happen if . . . ?" also is a traditional method for encouraging children to think about values and behavior.

The method is similar to brainstorming (next section) in that children are given an open-ended problem for which they list ideas. It can be used in a brainstorming setting ("What would happen if everyone were a thief? Think of all the ideas you can."). Or it can be used by parents or teachers as a short-term thought-provoking question: "The newspaper said that a sixth-grader was caught with a gun at school. What do you suppose would happen if EVERY kid carried a gun to school?" Or "What would happen if EVERYONE were rude to everyone else?"

Children and adolescents make lots of serious mistakes because "they did not think." They did not bother to predict and evaluate the outcomes, consequences, and implications of their behavior. As a tragic but horribly common example, without a moment's thought teenagers quickly shoot other teenagers—because of different gang membership. Young people are dead, their families devastated, and the shooter faces a prison sentence or sometimes execution. Do they think deeply about the consequences of their actions? *The purpose of "What would happen if . . . ?" exercises is to help children think about consequences of their behavior and examine why particular values and behavior are "good" or "bad" for others and themselves.*

"What would happen if teachers were always mean to children?"

"What would happen if the school were vandalized every night?"

"What would happen if we ignored drug dealers and let them sell drugs to children?"

Brainstorming and Reverse Brainstorming

Many teachers use *brainstorming* to "practice creativity" and to teach children about creative thinking. It can be used with nonsense problems ("How can we get that elephant out of the bathroom?") or serious problems ("How can we raise money for our field trip?" "How can we improve traffic safety?"). The method is simple. Children are asked to "Think of all the ideas you can" for a problem. They are encouraged to use their imaginations and even think of wild and far-fetched ideas, because wild ideas often can be changed into good ideas. During the idea generating session, participants are told not to criticize or evaluate ideas. The purpose is to produce a long list of ideas, and criticism interferes with the free flow. In typical classroom brainstorming, children learn that creativity and imagination are valued; that if they try, they *can* think of creative ideas; and that they should think of many ideas before selecting a final problem solution (Davis, 1992).

In the context of teaching values, the problems typically (not always) are sufficiently serious that *encouraging "wild" ideas is not recommended*. The goal is to stimulate children to think and reason—consciously, logically, and intelligently—about honesty, others' rights and feelings, rudeness, bad manners, drug use, the value of education, wastefulness, vandalism, and other productive or anti-social and self-destructive values, and why the values are good or bad, right or wrong. Serious stuff.

When children themselves think of reasons why a behavior is good or bad, or list ways to behave constructively instead of destructively, such thinking implicitly helps them make commitments to right action.

After introducing and briefly explaining a value, for example, *being pleasant*, and explaining or reviewing brainstorming procedures, children would be given a problem such as:

"Think of all the ways you can to be pleasant in the classroom"

"How can you cheer up your classmates? Think of all the ideas you can."

"How can you be more pleasant and helpful at home?"

"How can you make a new student feel welcome in our class?"

Reverse brainstorming is even more fun. With reverse brainstorming the problem statement is turned around: "Think of all the ways you can to be unpleasant." "How can we hurt other children's feelings? Think of all the ideas you can." "How many ways can we be rude to clerks in the stores?" The purpose of reverse brainstorming is not to provide inspiration for anti-social behavior. Rather, the procedure clarifies wrong behavior and its bad effects on others. *Reverse brainstorming usually reveals what people are, in fact, actually doing.*

Both types of brainstorming, and all other techniques in this book, should help children or adolescents *empathize* with victims of bad behavior, and thereby understand more deeply why a value or behavior is right or wrong, helpful or hurtful. They should come to think, "No, I would not want that to happen to me, and so it is wrong to do that to others."

Analogical Thinking

With analogical thinking children make imaginative comparisons. This approach includes a built-in humorous touch, yet it stimulates children to analyze serious attitudes and values. It resembles brainstorming and "What would happen if . . . ?" in being a group idea-listing strategy, although usually just a few ideas are suggested for each problem. As examples:

"How is being unfriendly like a squeaky clarinet?"

"How is being rude like a charging bull?"

"How is a good person like a good pizza?"

Again, these exercises typically do not last very long—perhaps 1 to 4 or 5 ideas will be suggested—and so the teacher (or parent) must be ready with follow-up discussion, additional analogy problems, or a related values activity.

Empathy: Taking Another Perspective

Empathy is taking another person's perspective, "putting yourself in their shoes," seeing things from a victim's point of view.

> The capacity to empathize probably is the single
> most important factor in moral thinking.

With empathy exercises, children are asked to imagine themselves in another person's role—usually the role of a person whose rights are being violated—and then imagine the feelings and thoughts of that person, as well as others involved.

In the follow-up, the teacher or parent discusses feelings, rights, how we like to be treated, how we should behave—and what we think of people who treat others badly. For example:

> Imagine you are Chris Alexander, a new person in the class. Everyone ignores you and some people make rude comments about your hair, your funny shoes, or your inability to work a math problem.
>
> How do you feel when others ignore you?
>
> How do you feel when others treat you rudely?
>
> Is it a good feeling? A bad feeling?
>
> What do we think of people who treat us rudely?
>
> How do you like others to treat you?
>
> How should we treat newcomers to our class?
>
> Are you the kind of person who will be rude and unpleasant to new students?
>
> Are you the kind of person who will help a newcomer feel welcome?

Visualization

The visualization activities are almost identical to Taking Another Perspective exercises. Both promote empathy. However, the visualization exercises are longer and children are asked to shut their eyes, relax, and let their imaginations come alive as the teacher reads the scenario. You ask children, as you read, to be thinking about right and wrong behavior and what they *should* do in these situations.

Most scenarios illustrate a bad attitude or value or undesirable behavior. Some stimulate imagery about the nice feelings associated with positive behavior, such as friendliness, helpfulness, doing favors, and doing a job well. You can make up original scenarios to fit values problems that your children are having, or that you anticipate they will have in coming years. As with all other exercises, a follow-up discussion centers on the meaning of the situation and the thoughts and feelings involved, and elicits commitments to positive behavior.

Questions and Discussion

Questions and discussion is a common teaching technique. In the present context it aims at raising children's awareness of why certain behaviors are desirable and others are not, and eliciting commitments to positive values and behavior. For example, a sequence might include: "What is rudeness?" "What are some examples of rudeness?" "Why is rudeness bad?" "How does it feel to be treated rudely?" "What do we think of rude people?" "Do you want people to think you are a rude person?" "*Should we be rude?*"

Conducting Classroom Sessions

The following is a recommended sequence for using any of the strategies described above. Parents, of course, may use these steps in a more personal, less formal way.

1. *Introducing the value.* The adult discusses the meaning of the particular value and how it relates, on one hand, to hurtful or destructive behavior or, on the other, to positive and constructive behavior. Real or hypothetical examples may be used. There should be emphasis on the perspectives, rights, and feelings of any person being mistreated—cheated, lied to, treated rudely, or whose property is vandalized or stolen—to stimulate empathy.

2. *Introducing the strategy.* The adult explains that "We are going to think about (a particular value) by using (a particular strategy)." The strategy is explained, step by step, along with the particular problem children will work on.

3. *Conducting the session.* The teacher and children use the strategy to raise awareness and understanding of the issue, and to elicit ideas,

reactions, and feelings. Ideally, children come to understand the value and make a personal commitment to constructive values and behavior.

4. *Follow-up*. After the session, the teacher leads a discussion of the meaning of the experience, reviewing with children how and why the particular value and behavior will hurt (or help) others, and how the value and behavior will hurt (or help) themselves. "How does it feel when . . . ?" and "What would happen if . . . ?" questions help stimulate empathy, understanding, and commitment.

In the follow-up, the adult also may wish to emphasize how such attitudes or behaviors make the perpetrator look "bad," "unable to think," or "self-centered" in the eyes of others. The adult also tries to elicit commitments to the particular value: "How many of you feel that showing respect to senior citizens and not being rude is a good idea?" "Are you the kind of person who will show respect and be polite to the elderly?" Self-respect and respect from others are emphasized. Long-term self-destructiveness also should be a focus.

After sessions using idea-generating strategies such as brainstorming, "What would happen if . . . ?", or problem solving, children can further reason and think logically about a value by *evaluating* the listed ideas. "Which ideas do you think are the most important?" "Which will work the best?" In reverse brainstorming, "Which ideas hurt people the most?" "Which ideas make us look like the worst thoughtless jerks?"

Small Group Option

With the "What would happen if . . . ?", Brainstorming, Reverse Brainstorming, and Analogical Thinking strategies, teachers can use small groups of 2, 3, or even 6 students. The teacher presents the problem, groups work on the problem for a few minutes, and then report their idea(s) to the class. Small groups can work on the same problem, or different groups can work on different problems.

In Theory . . .

Ideally, in relation to the Taxonomy of Affective Objectives summarized in Chapter 2, throughout all activities, exercises, and discussions, children (1) receive information about values, (2) respond to the values, and (hopefully) (3) accept the values, (4) organize the values within their larger sets of values, and (e) perhaps become characterized by the values. "Yes, I am a trustworthy, caring, and responsible person."

In relation to Kohlberg's stages of moral thinking, the goal is to help children "graduate" from Preconventional thinking, in which they are guided mindlessly by immediate rewards and punishments, at least into Conventional thinking about values, and perhaps into glimmerings of Postconventional thinking—self-chosen ethics based upon universal principles of justice and individual rights.

Reference

Davis, G. A. (1992). *Creativity is forever* (3rd Ed). Dubuque, IA: Kendall/Hunt.

5

Taking a Problem Solving Approach:

"What Is the Problem?" and "How Can We Solve It?"

It would be terrific if everyone took a "problem solving approach" to daily personal and job difficulties. It is a powerful thinking strategy that may be applied to most kinds of problems, including values problems. An effective problem solving approach requires just two main steps that are simple enough for young people to grasp: (1) **"What is the problem?"** (clarifying the problem) and (2) **"How can we solve it?"** (finding solutions). The second step includes thinking of lots of ideas, then selecting and implementing the best solution(s).

Taking a Problem Solving Approach is described only in this chapter. However, it can be applied by the teacher or parent to virtually any type of values issue. The Problem Solving Approach can be used as a values exercise itself. For example: "Kids are taking drugs. What is the problem here? . . . How can we solve it? What are some ideas?" In addition, the Problem Solving Approach makes an excellent follow-up exercise to help clarify a values issue and help children form commitments to positive values.

Clarifying The Problem: "What is the Problem?"

In this step the adult guides the child or children in understanding the problem. The focus is on helping the children understand *why* the behavior is bad—how it hurts others and ourselves. Especially, children should be helped to see a situation from a victim's point of view. They should understand what most people think of the inappropriate behavior. Children should agree that the poor value in question and the related behavior truly is a problem.

We mentioned in Chapter 1, and will see again in later chapters, that a big-time difficulty in the values and attitudes of young people is that they do not have *empathy*. They do not "see" a situation as others see it. They do not take others' points of view. They may not see an instance of dishonesty, rudeness, crime, vandalism, littering, or even murder as a "problem" in the same way that others do—particularly the victims. *A vital step in teaching values is helping children to truly understand the problem—to see a problematic situation as others see it.*

A teacher or parent would begin by explaining a "bad situation" or "bad behavior" in the school, family, or community. A question and answer format, as described in Chapter 4 and other question-and-discussion chapters, may be used to help children logically analyze and better comprehend the problem. For example, the adult can ask:

> Why is the situation "bad"? Why is it wrong?
>
> Who is hurt? You? Me? Everyone?
>
> Would you like this to happen to you? (Then should it happen to other people?)
>
> When does this happen?
>
> Where does it happen?
>
> Do we hurt ourselves when we do things like that? How?
>
> How are others in the school, family, or community hurt?
>
> What would happen if everyone did this?
>
> What do we think about people who do this?

You probably can add more *who, what, when, where, why,* and *how* questions that will help clarify the situation and how it is hurtful or damaging, and help children understand why the situation is indeed a problem.

Finding Solutions: "How Can We Solve It?"

In the second step children think of solutions to the problem—ideas for what can or should be done. It is a time-honored principle of social psychology that people who help make decisions are implicitly committed to those decisions. When children themselves think of solutions to a problem, there should be a strong commitment to those solutions—a commitment to better values and behavior.

Like the first step, this second step also requires children to think analytically and in a fair-minded way about a values problem and to make logical decisions about productive, caring behavior.

You may wish to think of this step as *brainstorming* and follow a brainstorming approach. The important brainstorming instruction is "Think of all the ideas you can." In a group situation, children also might be reminded not to criticize others' ideas—"because criticism is like punishment, and we don't want to punish each other for thinking of ideas."

In the classroom, the teacher (or a fast-writing student) records ideas on the chalkboard, where they are available for later review, comment, and evaluation.

If students have trouble getting started, or else they run out of ideas too quickly, the teacher can prime the idea pump with the following kinds of questions. (Think about littering, vandalism, stealing, or rudeness as examples of "problems.")

> What would be some examples of correct (not hurtful, harmful) behavior?
>
> What might a helpful, thoughtful person do? (Should we be helpful, caring people?)
>
> What would earn us respect from others?
>
> What might we do instead of (what is happening)? Would that be better?
>
> How might we help people who are making mistakes like this and are hurting others (and themselves)?
>
> How might we help them understand their hurtful/harmful behavior?
>
> How might we help them prefer better behavior?

How might we try to stop people from hurting others (and hurting themselves)?

How might we help the victims of the bad behavior.

It may take just 10 minutes or less for children to run out of ideas. But do not rush brainstorming; ideas become more original after the early, obvious ones are suggested.

After the list of ideas is produced, they may be evaluated informally by asking:

Which of these ideas might work the best?

Which of these ideas will best help solve the problem?

Which of these ideas are the most important?

Which will help the person the most?

Which would a thoughtful, considerate person do?

An informal consensus can be reached on one or two (or more) of the best ideas for solving the problem. Or a formal vote may be taken.

After the solution(s) are decided upon, if possible some action should be taken. For example, if the problem is littering the school hallways, trashing the restroom walls, or pilfering from lockers, the potential solutions could be transmitted to the principal. If the problem is classroom rudeness, messiness, or tardiness, the children can implement the chosen solution(s) themselves—which likely will be a commitment by everyone to shape up.

Time Required

In the classroom, treatment of a values/behavior problem may require 10 to 20 minutes, perhaps longer, to adequately analyze and clarify the situation, discuss possible solutions, evaluate and select the best ideas, and plan the agreed-upon courses of action.

Follow-Up

If solutions are selected, and action taken, no further follow-up may be needed. However, if you feel children do not yet grasp the problem or accept the solution(s), you may continue to clarify the problem and elicit commitments with additional probing questions such as:

Were you ever the victim of (the bad behavior)? How did you feel?

Have ever you seen or heard of (instances of the bad behavior?)

How do you think the victims (persons affected) felt?

Were they treated fairly?

Do thoughtful, caring people do that sort of thing?

Are you the sort of person who would do that?

6

Family Influence and Modeling, Peer Influence, TV and Movies

Becoming "Values Conscious"

A first step for parents and teachers is to become more "values conscious." Use every opportunity to point out to children how poor values can:

- Hurt others
- Hurt themselves
- Hurt their futures
- Hurt the environment
- Cause them to lose friends
- Cause them to lose respect from others
- Cause them to lose respect for themselves

Poor values underlie hurtful and self-destructive behavior. Positive values underlie caring and productive behavior.

Regrettably, there is no shortage of examples of behavior that reflects destructive values—in the news, in public places, and sometimes in the home and classroom. A short list of common behavior that reflects poor values might include:

Bad temper

Discourtesy

Unwillingness to help others

Rudeness

Breaking promises

Littering

Vandalizing

Petty theft, shoplifting

Undervaluing education and training

Dropping out of school

Mistreating the elderly

Mistreating disabled persons

Prejudice, bigotry, name calling

Bullying smaller children, younger siblings

Smoking, damaging ones health

Mistreating animals

Misbehaving in public

And for the really serious stuff:

Drug use

Murder

Robbery

Assault

Rape

Irresponsible sex

All of these provide substance for discussions, decisions and choices, and commitments about constructive values—about how to live. These are a few "follow up" questions that can be used to help clarify children's perceptions, thoughts, and feelings about real world values disasters.

Is that a good idea?

Why is that bad? Why is it wrong?

Who is hurt?

Should everybody do that?

Would the world be a better place if everyone did that?

Do we hurt others when we do that? How?

Do we hurt ourselves when we do that? How?

Does that hurt people? Is it good to hurt people?

Do we like to be hurt?

What would happen if everyone did that?

Would you like someone to do that to you?

Does that make the environment prettier or uglier?

Is "pretty" better than "ugly"?

What do we think of people who do things like that?

Would YOU do that?

Are YOU someone who would do that?

Such questions and discussions can help raise awareness of good and bad values and behavior; clarify *why* some behaviors are good and other behaviors are hurtful and destructive; and elicit commitments to good values and behavior.

Modeling: Parents

When children are young, parents are powerful role models. You have heard the phrase "So-and-so is setting a good/bad example for his/her children." Some "bad examples" are parents who:

Shoplift

Express bigotry

Express contempt for school and education

Leave messes at picnic areas

Disarrange shelves and displays in stores

Quickly become rude or violent

Drive fast and recklessly

Use drugs

Such parents cause their children to believe that such habits are acceptable, even desirable. Perhaps you have heard this semi-humorous anecdote: "I'll teach you to hit your sister! Take that ✳! And that ✳! And that ✳!" In a recent Madison, Wisconsin, news report, a mother helped her son hold down, beat, and slash a smaller child who had tried to retrieve his bicycle stolen by the son. This mom is not a good role model.

The vast majority of parents do not *deliberately* teach their children values that are negative or destructive. Parents also may not *deliberately* teach values that are positive and constructive. But parents can and do teach values of both varieties. The following list presents some examples of how parents can model constructive values. If you have taken the trouble to obtain and read this book, you probably are doing most or all of them already. If so, the list will serve only as a reminder.

✓ Keep promises. Comment to your children that "Keeping promises tells others you are trustworthy."

✓ Let your children know that you always return things that you borrow. Let children hear you thank the person(s) who loaned you the things.

✓ Never steal in stores. Anything. Not a peanut. Mention that "Stealing hurts others," "You don't like your things stolen, do you?", and "People who steal are dishonest and untrustworthy creeps." A child who watches mom, uncle Harry, or the neighbors loot stores during a riot or power blackout is a future looter.

✓ Don't make messes in grocery, drug, or department stores. If a bag of noodles is on the floor, most people will step over it. Pick it up and put it back on the shelf. Your children will be impressed that you have shown more concern than have others.

✓ Remind children *frequently* that the best—or ONLY—way to "make a good living" is to get an education and professional/technical training. Use yourself, relatives, neighbors as examples. Point out examples of persons—perhaps older teenagers or young couples—who dropped out of school or have no professional training, and are either unable to find a job or are not adequately employed. Ask "Would you like to be unable to find a good job and make a good living when you are older?"

Girls as well as boys must accept as a "given" that education and training are essential: Two incomes per family often are necessary, and high divorce rates make job training for females critical.

✓ On the topic of money, the old sayings "Money can't buy happiness" and "Money isn't everything" are true, of course. But you must help children and youth realize that being able to earn money is VITAL. At the very least, money is necessary for a place to live, food, clothes, probably a car, and a little entertainment once in a while. Most people want more than "the very least." Most people want a nice place to live and sufficient funds for comforts and opportunities above bare-bones survival.

✓ Model the "Just do the best you can" or "Give it the old college try" attitude. Too many children (and adults) avoid beneficial educational and other experiences because they fear they will not do well. A parent can model "give it a try" attitudes with such comments as: "Well, I'm not sure I can install that new ceiling fan myself, but I'm going to do the best I can." "I'm not very good at art, but I think I'll take that beginning art class at the technical college anyway. I'll just do the best I can." "I'm a lousy at volleyball, but it's fun to try to play. I'll just do the best I can and not worry about it."

✓ Show respect for teachers and school administrators, and emphasize the value of doing ones best in school. A dad who says "School work is a waste of time," ". . . for girls," or ". . . for sissies" is guaranteeing that his son will underachieve in school.

In school, sports and extracurricular activities are good experiences and make school more enjoyable. However, parents who value only athletics and/or popularity—to the exclusion of studying and grades—also will cause their children to underachieve and develop perhaps too-modest career aspirations.

✓ When vandalizing (spray painting, broken windows) or messes at parks and picnic areas are seen, comment that such behavior makes the world uglier, and that "People who do this have no respect for others' property or others' right to an attractive environment." An excellent habit, and a good value to convey to children, is to leave picnic areas *cleaner* than you found them.

✓ Show respect for the elderly, especially grandparents and senior citizens in the neighborhood. Do them favors; help with strenuous chores such as shoveling snow or moving heavy things.

✓ Accept individual differences. Comment often that "people of all races live in America, and everybody deserves fair and decent treatment." Your children should never hear you criticize persons who are overweight, underweight, too tall, too short, disabled, disfigured, of another race or religion, or poor, or call them unflattering names.

Like all values and ethics, bigotry and prejudice are learned from adults and peers.

✓ Take found articles to the "Lost and Found." Mention that "If we lose something, it sure is nice if people turn it in!"

✓ Display good manners—always! At home, in stores, in restaurants, on buses, and when visiting friends or relatives. If you want thoughtful, considerate children, you must yourself show thoughtful, considerate behavior. Say "Please," "Thank you," and "Excuse me." Open doors for others, especially the elderly. Pick up things for people when they drop them. Send "Thank You" notes. And so forth.

✓ Don't be pushy, rude, or belligerent with store clerks, waiters and waitresses, bus drivers, teachers, school administrators, or others. Show pleasantness and respect. Comment that "We like to be treated with pleasantness and respect, and so we should treat others that way." You can mention also that, "If we have a proper complaint, we can get our point across without being rude, pushy, or obnoxious."

> Reminder: Lecturing at children to "behave" is far less effective than helping them independently understand and embrace constructive values and behavior. Parents, like teachers, are respected models who can teach good values by modeling good values.

Modeling: Teachers

Most of the above suggestions are suitable for classroom use. As a teacher, you probably already try to model patience, politeness, neatness, honesty, using proper English, putting trash in trash cans, and the like. You demonstrate (and sometimes enforce) promptness, raising hands before speaking, taking turns, sharing, beginning requests with "May I . . . ," doing favors, taking things to the Lost and Found, and so forth.

You realize that children cannot read your mind, and so you often *tell* them what you are doing and why. You also use classroom, school, and community episodes as opportunities to discuss helpful and hurtful values (or "citizenship"). A recommended philosophy is to help the children (1) evaluate the pros and cons of poor behavior, (2) decide that positive behavior (and values) are better, and (3) make a thoughtful commitment to positive values.

"Juan, would you run this down to the Lost and Found in the main office? When we lose things, do we like to get them back? Do we like people to turn them in?"

"Tonight I'm going to help my neighbor cut her lawn. She is an elderly lady and lives alone. Do you think it makes her happy when I help her? Is it a good idea to help neighbors who are senior citizens?"

"Joe promised to clean the erasers after school today. Should Joe keep his promise? Do trustworthy people keep their promises? Is it good to be trustworthy?"

"I saw some awful spray painting on the building this morning! What kind of people do that? Are they thoughtful? Considerate? Are they making the building prettier or uglier? Which is best, pretty or ugly?"

"Some children are not using trash cans. They are tossing papers and candy wrappers all over the halls and playground. Does this make the halls prettier for everyone? Does this make the playground prettier? Is it fair to make other people clean up our messes? Would you like to have to clean up messes that other children make?"

"I saw a couple of fifth-graders smoking this morning. Is smoking good for you? Is smoking smelly and expensive? Is our health important? Is anything more important? What happens if we do not take care of our health?"

"Someone in this room was being rude to another person. Do we like people to be rude to us? Should we be nasty and unpleasant and rude to other people?"

"Shonita's calculator was stolen from her desk yesterday. I feel very bad when this happens. How do you feel when something of yours is stolen? Is it good to steal other children's things?"

"I was talking to some teachers from Washington High School. They told me that many teenagers are dropping out of school. Without an education they can't get a job. And they get into trouble with the law. Is dropping out of school a good idea? Is it better to stay in school? And to get good job training?"

Offsetting Negative Home Values

Teachers sometimes must try to offset the damaging effects of parents or older siblings who model unproductive, self-destructive values and attitudes. For example, in some blue-collar or poor families parents and older siblings may not value education. They may expect their children to get jobs similar to their parents' jobs after high school, and these expectations are transmitted to the children. The words "college" or "technical school" are not heard at home. We noted above that parents' anti-school and anti-achievement attitudes are picked up by children and lead to underachievement and low career aspirations.

Some parents teach, by modeling, the poor values listed at the beginning of this chapter, from bad temper, rudeness, and littering to drug use, looting, and shooting people.

Discussing with parents how to model good values can help. Modeling by you, the teacher, along with exercises and activities in this book and in *Values Are Forever* also can help offset damaging home values.

Peer Influence

It is no secret that when children become teenagers, conformity becomes rampant. Everybody dresses the same, talks the same, and listens to the same music. In recent years it's been baggy clothes, expensive athletic shoes that are never tied (the brand depends on the school), and sometimes sidewall haircuts for boys. If the peers are honest kids with civilized social skills and positive education and career aspirations—no problem. If the peers are budding criminals and likely dropouts—*problem*!

For parents, a loving home that embraces values of caring, responsibility, and education usually can offset negative influences of teen peers. Not always. However, when the teenagers' parents and other relatives embrace the same delinquent and criminal attitudes as the peers . . . well, that's why America has a horrifying values problem.

Much better brains than your author's have tried to find solutions to today's problems of teenagers dropping out of school, taking and selling drugs, terrorizing neighborhoods, and killing others because of wrong gang membership or traffic arguments.

Occasionally, solutions such as midnight basketball games, gymnastics, and choral groups work miracles and make national news, but these only help a tiny fraction of problem teenagers. The most touted solutions are "Build more prisons" and "Lower the age at which teens can be tried as adults."

For all young people—those in advantaged and disadvantaged circumstances—the best and perhaps only workable solution is to begin teaching values when kids are young and will listen. Perhaps they will grasp how some values and behavior will trash their lives. Other values and behavior will help them live more comfortable, happier lives. Early values training might inoculate at least some children against families and teenage peers who promote stealing, drug dealing, terrorizing neighbors, and even murder, and who proclaim that school and career preparation are a waste of time.

And we cannot forget a gazillion other positive values that pre-teen children need to understand and embrace, values related to their current and future well-being and to others' rights and feelings—good health, trustworthiness, responsibility, caring attitudes, democracy and fair play, empathy, and so forth.

To the extent possible, teach your children and your students that when they become teenagers, they will influenced by other teens. They will want to be liked, and so they will do, say, and even think what the others say is "correct." Some things that other teenagers do can damage their health (smoking, drugs) or their future lives (stealing, joining gangs, dropping out). They must be careful NOT to let other teenagers harm their lives. They must make their *own* decisions and choices.

TV and Movies

Debates have raged and much research exists on the influence of television and movies on children's values. The consensus seems to be that, yes, children (mostly boys) can and DO learn from TV that violence is an acceptable way to solve problems, and that REAL men (the heroes) beat up and kill people (the bad guys, who are not us). Saturday cartoons have been dubbed "The Saturday Morning Massacre" for good reason. Besides violence, the other half of the TV influence debate centers on sex. No passionate lover on TV or in a movie ever said, "Wait, stop! We need to use a condom!" or "Hold it, we could get AIDS and die!" or "Let's just have an ice cream cone and talk!"

This book is not about sex education, which today is AIDS education. Community values influence what can and cannot be covered in local elementary classrooms. For now, let's just agree that NOT getting AIDS is a life-or-death value, one that must be taught at least in the home, if not in the schools, churches, on billboards, and on television. If a teacher or parent wished, some exercises in this book (e.g., "What would happen if . . . ?") could be modified to help children *understand* this value and make *commitments* to avoiding AIDS.

MTV can teach girls to over-value being sexy, and teach both boys and girls to over-value dancing skill and discos. If (heaven forbid!) anyone took *Beavis and Butt Head* seriously, these characters teach bad language and crudeness and that females are sex objects, defiance of adults is terrific, and stupidity in school is funny. At least one parent known to this author blames MTV and *Beavis and Butt Head*, in part, for her two adolescent boys' rude and rebellious behavior. Behavior not learned from their gracious and educated mother nor their parochial school. Programs such as Saturday cartoons and late-night MTV, including *Beavis and Butt Head*, can be entertaining. But children should understand that many values displayed on these shows are NOT ones that children should adopt. Be direct. Present ideas such as: "These shows are fun to watch, but they can teach values that might hurt you!

Comment

Whether the source of some destructive values is TV violence or pressure to "be cool and join the Gangster Gang," inoculation is in order. Use examples from the school, the community, or ones that make the news to discuss how poor values and behavior can hurt others, hurt ourselves, and even trash our lives. Use discussion and some of the "What would happen if . . . ?", brainstorming, and visualization exercises in this idea book to convince kids that "In the next 10 years you will see lots of BAD values, especially on TV and in teenage friends. DON'T BE FOOLED! DON'T BE TAKEN IN! Bad values can and will wreck your life! Don't let them mess up your head."

Part III

Honesty, Trustworthiness

Chapter

7

"What Would Happen If ...

Everyone Were a Thief?"

Defining "Honesty"?

Like most values discussed in this workbook, we know honesty and dishonesty when we see them, and we know that dishonesty hurts people. Our *Funk and Wagnall's* defines *honest* as "fair, truthful, honorable, and trustworthy." *Trustworthy* is defined as "dependable, reliable, of high integrity, and honest." For present purposes, *honesty* includes:

Not stealing

Not cheating

Not vandalizing

Not lying

Returning things that are borrowed

Keeping promises

Can you think of other categories of "honesty" or "dishonesty"?

Objectives

A major contributor to misbehavior, delinquency, and seemingly amoral thinking is that young people do not think about the *consequences* of their actions. The purpose of "What would happen if . . . ?" exercises is to practice "thinking ahead"— thinking about the negative consequences of wrongful, hurtful values and behavior, and the positive consequences of constructive values and behavior.

The purpose of "What would happen if . . . ?" activities in this chapter is to:

Help children understand and make commitments to the principle that honesty is better than dishonesty, trustworthy is better than untrustworthy—for others and themselves.

Help children value being judged an honest, trustworthy person.

Help children form identities as honest, trustworthy people.

Time Required

"What would happen if . . . ?" exercises do not take long, perhaps 3 to 10 minutes each, depending upon the particular problem and children's interest. Of course, introductions and follow-up discussion add to the time requirement.

Getting Started

Discuss the meaning of the particular value—in this section, *honesty* and *trustworthiness*—with emphasis on how we need to think about the consequences of our actions and the effects upon others and ourselves. You might mention, for example, how we feel when our things are stolen or when people borrow our things and do not return them.

Explain that "We are going to think about what happens as a result of dishonest behavior. We are going to think about other people's feelings and other things that happen as a result of being dishonest and untrustworthy."

Explain that "The problem will begin with 'What would happen if . . . ?'. You can use your imaginations and think about what happens when people do certain things or behave in certain ways. Everybody understand? Good!"

With "What would happen if . . . ?", Brainstorming, Reverse Brainstorming, and analogical thinking, the teacher should record ideas on the chalkboard where they will be available for modification, combination, avoiding duplication, and for later review and comment. A fast-writing student volunteer may be the "scribe" when the class becomes familiar with the group-think procedures.

Note also that these techniques—"What would happen if . . . ?", Brainstorming, Reverse Brainstorming, and Analogical Thinking problems—can be used in a small group format. Groups of 2 to 6 children can think of ideas for a given problem and then make a group report to the class. Groups can work on exactly the same problem or different groups can be assigned different problems.

Guiding The Session

Children are quick to focus on the consequences of honesty and dishonesty—"We might get caught," "They would get mad at us," "We might get spanked," "We might get sent to the principal's office," or "Mom won't let me watch TV." This is normal and acceptable. However, you should guide the discussion to higher levels of moral thinking by asking, for example: "Does being dishonest hurt other people?" "Does being dishonest hurt ourselves?" "What do we think of people who are dishonest?" "Do we want them for friends?" "What do people think of us when are dishonest (when we lie, cheat, steal, destroy property, or don't return things)?" "Is it really a good idea to be a dishonest person?"

If there are silent spots in "What would happen if . . ." problems (or Brainstorming, Reverse Brainstorming, or Analogy problems), the teacher can solicit ideas from quieter children or suggest ideas of his or her own. Sometimes, ideas may be stimulated by suggesting specific contexts or situations, for example, in school, in the classroom, during art or music, in the cafeteria, at home, in the neighborhood, in shopping centers, downtown, on the bus, visiting relatives, when playing games, and so forth.

Follow-Up

After, or during, a "What would happen if . . . ?" activity, the teacher or parent can use leading questions to stimulate thought and discussion. The purpose of these follow-up activities is to help children further understand the value of honesty and the damage to others or themselves caused by dishonesty. Try to maximize understanding and empathy. Try to elicit a commitment to the idea that "honesty is better than dishonesty" and "I want to be an honest, trustworthy person."

Some possible *clarification* questions are:

How would things be different?

What would school be like?

What would home be like?

What would your friends be like?

What would YOU be like?

What would the community be like?

Would the community be a better place to live?

You can help elicit *commitment* to honesty as a personal value with:

Is it important for our friends and family to trust us? Why?

Why is (a particular outcome) important?

Would you be a better person if you did this?

Would you be proud of yourself?

Would you have more self-respect?

Does dishonesty hurt others?

Does dishonesty hurt ourselves?

What do we think of people who are dishonest?

Do we want them for friends?

What do people think of US when we lie, cheat, steal, destroy things, or don't return things? Do they think we are really swell people?

Does vandalism make things uglier or prettier? Which is better?

Is it a wonderful idea to be a dishonest person?

Are you the type of person who is honest?

"What Would Happen If . . . ?" Problems About Honesty and Trustworthiness

Problem 7.1	**What would happen if everyone were a thief—your parents, brothers, sisters, neighbors, teachers, store clerks, and everybody else?** They all steal everything they can get their hands on! What would happen?
Problem 7.2	**What would happen if NO ONE were a thief?** Everyone is honest—your parents, brothers, sisters, neighbors, teachers, store clerks, and everybody else. What would happen?

Problem 7.3   **What would happen if everybody cheated in every way they possibly could?** Everybody cheats in softball games and other games. Everybody tries to cheat on spelling and arithmetic tests. Everybody tries to grab more than their share of everything. What would happen?

Problem 7.4   **What would happen if NOBODY ever cheated in any way?** Nobody cheats in games. Nobody cheats on tests. Nobody tries to take more than their share of everything. What would happen?

Problem 7.5   **What would happen if every shop owner, every store clerk, and every cab driver tried to cheat every customer they had?**

Problem 7.6   **What would happen if everybody decided to be a shoplifter?** What would stores be like? What would the world be like? What would YOU be like?

Problem 7.7   **What would happen if NOBODY ever stole anything from stores?** How would stores be different? How would people be different?

Problem 7.8   **What would happen if the school were vandalized every night?** Windows are broken, flower beds and grass are dug up. Classrooms are burglarized and damaged and things are stolen. What would happen? What would school be like? What would people think?

Problem 7.9   **What would happen if NOBODY ever vandalized anything?** Nobody breaks window, damages cars, spray paints buildings or bus stops, or cuts garden hoses. How would the world be different?

Problem 7.10   **What would happen if nobody ever told the truth?** Everybody always told lies! You couldn't believe anything anybody said. What would home be like? What would school be like? What would stores be like?

Problem 7.11   **What would happen if nobody ever returned anything they borrowed?** They just borrowed things and then kept them!

Problem 7.12   **What would happen if everyone always returned things they borrowed, on time and in perfect condition?** Would that be great?

Problem 7.13   **What would happen if no one ever kept their promises?** How would things be different? Would things be better?

Problem 7.14   **What would happen if everybody always kept their promises?** How would things be different? Would things be better?

Problem 7.15   **What would happen if we couldn't trust ANYBODY?** If nobody at all were trustworthy?

Problem 7.16   **What would happen if we could trust everyone?** Every person you meet is absolutely trustworthy? Would the world be a better place?

Chapter

8

Brainstorming About Honesty:

"Why Should We Be Honest?"

About Brainstorming

As described in Chapter 4, the mechanics of brainstorming are simple: Children are asked to "Think of all the ideas you can" for a problem and are encouraged to use their imaginations. They are asked not to criticize or evaluate ideas. The purpose of brainstorming is to produce a long list of ideas, and criticism interferes with imagination.

In the context of teaching values, brainstorming helps children *think* about a particular values problem; *understand* the consequences of behavior stemming from a particular value; *make a conscious decision* about whether the value and related actions are helpful or hurtful; and *make commitments* pertaining to the value.

Objectives

As with "What would happen if . . . ?" problems: To help children value honesty, make commitments to honesty, value being judged a trustworthy person, and form identities as honest, trustworthy persons.

Time Required

Brainstorming usually elicits more ideas that "What would happen if . . . ?" problems, and so time expectations can range from 5 to 8 minutes at the brief end, to 10 or 15 minutes on the lengthy side. Some problems will be more exciting than others, and therefore elicit greater engagement and more ideas. Introductions and follow-up discussion also will require a few minutes.

Getting Started

Introduce the meaning of *honesty* or a specific type or example of honesty or dishonesty. For example, ask children "What do we mean by *honesty*?" "What do we mean by *dishonesty*?"

Then explain that "We are going to think about honesty and dishonesty by using brainstorming. Instead of raining rain, we're going to rain ideas!"

Explain or review the brainstorming rules:

✓ We will think of all the ideas we can. We want a long list of ideas. I'll write them on the board.

✓ We won't criticize each other's ideas, because criticism is like punishment.

You may can paraphrase and elaborate each problem question any way you wish. For example, in Problem 7.1 children are asked to think of examples of honesty. You might probe for ideas by asking, "What kinds of honesty do you see at school?" "In your neighborhood?" "When playing games?"

If children run out of ideas, ask the quieter children if they have an idea. You also can make suggestions of your own.

A small-group format, including group reports of ideas, also may be used.

Guiding The Session

As with "What would happen if . . . ?" problems, children will tend to focus on low-level consequences of honesty or dishonesty: "We might get spanked," "We might get sent to the principal's office," or "Somebody will get sore at us." Whenever possible guide the discussion to higher levels of thinking about values: "Does being dishonest hurt others?" "Hurt ourselves?" "What do we think of dishonest people?" "What do people think of US when we are dishonest?" *"Should we be dishonest people?"*

Follow-Up

There are many possibilities for thought-prodding follow-up questions that can help children better understand the benefits of honesty and the hurtfulness of dishonesty. Try to maximize *understanding, empathy* and *commitment*: "How does someone feel when a favorite possession is stolen?" "Are we are the type of people who will be honest?"

With a focus on *honesty*:

Which of these ideas (on the chalkboard) are the most important? Why?

Which ideas make us look like we care about other people? (All of them? Why?)

Which ideas make us look intelligent and thoughtful?

Is it important for our friends and family to trust us? Why?

How are we better off by being honest?

Are you the type of person who is honest?

With a focus on *dishonesty*:

Which of these things hurt people the most? Why?

Which ideas make us look selfish, like we don't care about anybody but ourselves? Why?

Are dishonest people good to have as friends?

What do we think of people who do these things?

Would you like your friends, your family, or your neighbors to believe you are a dishonest person? What do you think about that?

What happens to teenagers and adults who steal cars, become burglars, or steal ladies purses? Would you like that to happen to you?

What would we think of ourselves if we were dishonest?

Are you the type of person who would do these things?

Are you a dishonest person?

Brainstorming Problems About Honesty and Dishonesty

Problem 8.1   What are some examples of being honest? How can we be honest people? In what ways can we show people that we are honest? Let's think of all the ideas we can.

Problem 8.2   Why should we be honest? List all of the ideas you can think of?

Problem 8.3   What are some examples of being dishonest? Can you think of some examples of stealing, breaking promises, lying, cheating, destroying property (vandalizing), or not returning things that we borrow? Have you seen some of these dishonest things? (Be sure to ask children not to use classmates as examples!)

Problem 8.4   How have we been hurt by dishonesty? Have you had things stolen? Have people cheated you? Have people not returned things? Have people broken their promises to you? Let's make a list of how we have been hurt by dishonesty. (Again, no names!)

Problem 8.5   Let's brainstorm nicknames a boy or girl who is often dishonest? We'll just make up some names. (Hints: "Larry the liar," "Vivian the vandal," "Ronald the rotten person," "Cheryl the shoplifter," "Charley the Cheater," etc.. Again, fictitious.)

Problem 8.6   How many ways can you think of that people sometimes cheat? (Hints: Games, sports, spelling tests, income tax, crowding in line, . . .)

Problem 8.7   How many ways can you think of that people (like you or me) are hurt by others stealing?

Problem 8.8   Instead of stealing something from a store, like a candy bar, a cassette tape, or a CD, how many honest ways can you think of to get something you really want?

Problem 8.9   How many examples of vandalism can we think of? Vandalism means deliberately breaking other people's things, spray painting, writing on walls, and generally destroying other people's property. What examples of vandalism have you seen? (Hints: At school, on or in public buildings, at bus stops, inside buses, in rest rooms.)

Problem 8.10 How many reasons can you think of why vandalism (breaking, destroying, spray painting) things at school, in public buildings, or elsewhere is bad? That is, what happens after young people destroy things that are not theirs?

Problem 8.11 Imagine that Joe Smith is in the habit of lying—he lies about everything. What will happen to Joe as a result of all this lying?

Problem 8.12 Why is it good to return things that you borrow. Think all of the ideas you can.

Problem 8.13 How many ways can you think of that people can break promises?

Problem 8.14 Imagine that Bill Jones is a drug dealer. He sells harmful drugs to children. How is Bill Jones being dishonest and hurtful? Think of all the ideas you can.

Reverse Brainstorming About Honesty:

"How Many Ways Can We Vandalize?"

Reverse Brainstorming

Reverse brainstorming usually is fun—it's hard to be serious when you are trying to think of ways to make a problem WORSE. It is common in reverse brainstorming for people to suggest ideas that, in fact, reflect what already is happening. For example, if a group of teachers were asked to brainstorm ideas for "How can our community *promote* vandalism?", probably every answer would reflect what actually is happening to promote vandalism.

Objectives

We don't truly want children to become more rude and delinquent. The purpose of reverse brainstorming is to engage children in thinking about a values issue, stimulate logical thinking about the value, and make commitments to the opposite, constructive value.

Time Required

As with regular brainstorming, 5 to 8 minutes on the short side, to maybe 10 or 15 minutes if the problem is a rousing one. Plus a few minutes for introductions and follow-up discussions.

Getting Started

Explain that "We are going to have some fun thinking about values. We are going to turn brainstorming around. We are going to use Reverse Brainstorming. (Does everyone know what 'reverse' means?) Instead of thinking of ways to make our values and behavior better, we are going to think of all the ways we can to make something WORSE. Sometimes we can understand a problem better by turning it around. For example, instead of thinking of ways to keep hallways clean, we think about ways to make them messier! We want a long list of ideas. We won't or criticize others' ideas, because criticism is like punishment."

As with Brainstorming, the teacher or a student will record ideas on the chalkboard, where they will be available for follow-up discussion.

Again, a small-group format followed by a group report may be used.

Guiding the Session

The teacher (or parent) can stimulate ideas by suggesting contexts, for example, in school, at home, visiting relatives, at friends' homes, in stores and shopping centers, on the streets, in buses, when playing games, and so forth.

Follow-Up

With reverse brainstorming, a follow-up is essential. Children must acknowledge and accept the obvious—that these ideas are what we should NOT do.

Always, try to maximize *understanding* and *empathy*, and try to elicit *commitments* to healthy, constructive attitudes.

Discussion questions similar to those in "What would happen if . . . ?" problems and brainstorming might ask:

Which of these ideas would work the best (make us look the most dishonest)? Why?

Which ideas make us look like we really, really don't care about other people and their feelings? (All of them? Why?)

Which of these things might hurt people the most? Why?

Is it good to hurt people? Do WE like to be hurt?

How do we feel when people steal things from us?

How do we feel when people cheat in games? What do we think of people who cheat in games?

How do we feel when some thoughtless person deliberately damages or destroy's our things? Maybe somebody steps on your lunch, scratches your bicycle or deliberately breaks your pencils. How does this make you feel? (Angry? Hurt? Sad?)

Which ideas make us look intelligent and thoughtful? None of them? Why?

Do some of these ideas make us look selfish, like we don't care about anybody but ourselves? Which ones?

What kind of people are dishonest? Are they intelligent? Thoughtful? Considerate?

Are dishonest people good to have as friends?

What do we think of people who actually do these things?

Would you like your friends, your family, or your neighbors to believe you destroy other people's property?

Would you like your friends or your family to never loan you anything—because they know you won't return what you borrow?

Is it important for people to trust us?

What will we think of ourselves if we are dishonest?

How are we better off by being honest?

Are you the type of person who would do these things?

Are you a dishonest, untrustworthy person?

Are you an honest, trustworthy person?

Reverse Brainstorming About Honesty and Trustworthiness

Problem 9.1   Imagine that we WANT people to think we are dishonest, untrustworthy people! How many ways can we think of to show that we just not to be trusted? What could we do to prove to people that we are truly dishonest?

Problem 9.2   How many different things can you borrow and not return—so that people will think you are a real crummy person? Let's think of all the ideas we can.

Problem 9.3   Imagine that we are playing softball. Pretend that our class is one team, and we are playing against a team from another class. How many ways can we think of to cheat in a softball game? Use your imaginations.

Problem 9.4   Imagine that we just love to vandalize and destroy people's property. How many ways can we think of to hurt people by vandalizing, wrecking, or spray painting people's property or public property?

Problem 9.5   How can we make it easy for people to steal our things?

Problem 9.6   How can we hurt people by being dishonest? List all the ideas you can think of. (Note: This activity is similar to Problem 9.1, and might best be used on a different day.)

Problem 9.7   How many ways can we break promises? Let's think of lots of ways to make promises, and then break them!

Problem 9.8   How can we hurt ourselves by being dishonest?

Analogical Thinking:

"How Is an Honest Person Like a Good Pizza?"

Analogical Thinking

When we think analogically we make comparisons. Analogical thinking is a good teaching and learning strategy. For example, knowing that an African *dingo* is like a *dog* immediately helps one understand the dingo.

Objectives

To stimulate analogical comparisons involving honest or dishonest behavior. Such comparisons should help children think about and make decisions regarding why some behavior is desirable and other behavior is hurtful to others and themselves.

Time Required

Each exercise may last just a minute or two, perhaps a few seconds. The teacher (or parent) should be ready with a follow-up discussion, additional analogy problems, or another activity. However, do not allow a session to end too quickly—encourage children to "put on your thinking caps" and "dig deeper" for comparisons.

Getting Started

Discuss the meaning of an *analogy* as a comparison, looking for similarities. You might use poetic or other examples. For example, clouds are like cotton, a calm lake is like a mirror, happiness is like a warm puppy, a roller coaster ride is like falling, a tiger is like a pet cat, a continent is like an island.

Explain that "We are going to think about honesty and trustworthiness by using analogies, by comparing honesty to other things." Encourage children to use their creative imaginations to come up with as many comparisons as they can.

Introduce the problem: "How is a _____ like a _____ ?" If someone makes a comparison that is unclear, you may explain the comparison yourself or ask the person to explain how "A" is similar to "B."

Be sure to record ideas on the chalkboard or have a student volunteer do so.

In a small-group format, groups of 2 to 6 can brainstorm answers to the question, then make a group report to the class. Groups may work on the same or different analogical problems.

Follow-Up

After each analogy problem, review the comparisons, emphasize and explain the particular points of similarity. For example, someone might suggest that "An honest, trustworthy person is like a good pizza because we like them both." You would emphasize and explain the comparison, perhaps adding that "We do not particularly like bad pizzas or people who cheat us or steal our things, do we."

There are many other possibilities for follow-up exercises. For example:

1. The teacher can ask children to make up their own analogies. On the chalkboard write, "**An honest person** (or a helpful person, a friendly person, a polite person, a good friend; or a person who cheats, steals, is rude, is a bully, is impolite, loses his/her temper, wastes supplies, never shares, never helps at home, makes messes for others to clean up, etc.) **is like** _____." Children can volunteer answers in an oral exercise. Or they can spend 5 or 10 minutes writing answers at their desks or tables, then report them.

2. A teacher or parent also can improvise novel analogical comparisons on the spot. For example, "**How is a criminal like** (a sick computer, stampeding elephant, broken clock, squeaky clarinet, rattlesnake, stack of Monopoly money)?"

3. For a quick follow-up, some of the present exercises can be reversed:

   "How is a *dis*honest person like a *bad* pizza?"

   "How is a *dis*honest person like a pair of jeans that *doesn't* fit right?"

   "How is an *un*trustworthy person like a *broken* bicycle?"

4. The two parts of the present analogies can be recombined:

   Corky the criminal is a bank robber. How is Corky like a hungry shark? (10.4 + 10.7)

   How is a person who cheats in a game (like Monopoly) like a mosquito? (10.5 + 10.6)

   Charlie Cheater cheats at everything. How is Charlie like a sinking ship? (10.6 + 10.4)

   How is someone who steals things out of your desk like a rock in your shoe? (10.7 + 10.5)

   Shirley Shoplifter stuffs things in her pocket every time she goes into a store. How is Shirley like a robot with its wires mixed up? (10.8 + 10.9)

   How is Dan the Vandal like a case of the measles? (10.9 + 10.8)

As always, be sure the value or behavior, and the reasons it is good or hurtful, are clear. Emphasize the point of view of any victim(s), and try to elicit commitments to positive attitudes and behavior.

   Is it good to be dishonest? Why?

   What kind of people are dishonest? Do they think about others' rights?

   Do dishonest people make good friends?

   What would we think of ourselves if we were dishonest?

   Is it better to be honest?

   Will people trust us if we are honest?

   Is it good for people to trust us? Is it good to be trustworthy?

   Are you an honest, trustworthy person?

Analogical Thinking Problems About Honesty

Problem 10.1	How is an honest, trustworthy person like a good pizza?
Problem 10.2	How is an honest, trustworthy person like a comfortable old pair of jeans?
Problem 10.3	How is a trustworthy person like a good bicycle?
Problem 10.4	Corky the criminal is a bank robber. How is Corky like a sinking ship?
Problem 10.5	How is a person who cheats in a game (like Monopoly) like a rock in your shoe?
Problem 10.6	Imagine that Charlie Cheater cheats at everything—games, spelling tests, and grabbing the biggest piece of pie. He'll try to give you two nickels and a dime in change for a quarter. How is Charlie like a mosquito?
Problem 10.7	How is someone who steals things out of your desk (locker) like a hungry shark? (Don't forget that sharks have tiny brains!)
Problem 10.8	Shirley Shoplifter stuffs things in her pocket every time she goes into a store. How is Shirley like a good case of the measles?
Problem 10.9	Dan the Vandal thinks it's great fun to write things with spray paint on fences, buildings, and bus stop shelters. Sometimes, he breaks windows and smashes kids' toys. How is Dan the Vandal like a robot with its wires mixed up?
Problem 10.10	How is vandalizing your school like sticking your finger in a pencil sharpener?
Problem 10.11	Lisa the Liar fibs about everything. She said her mother is a "famous author" and "won an Olympic Gold Medal in swimming." She also said "I won a chess tournament when I was 7 years old," and "My family is going to Russia next summer!" She always lies about things she borrows, so she can keep them. She says, "I didn't borrow it" or "I already returned it." How is Lisa the Liar like a McDonald's hamburger without any meat or catsup in it?

Problem 10.12 How is someone who tells a lot of lies like play (Monopoly) money?

Problem 10.13 How is returning things that you borrow like a trip to an amusement park (or theme park, or some place else fun)?

Problem 10.14 If you don't return things you borrow, how are you like an iron magnet?

Problem 10.15 How is breaking promises like a rotten tomato?

Problem 10.16 How is keeping promises like a pretty sunset?

Taking Another Perspective:

"How Does It Feel To Be a Dishonest Creep?"

Taking Another Perspective: Empathy

As mentioned earlier, a core problem with misbehaving young people is that they do not take other people's perspectives. They do not see their inappropriate or hurtful behavior as others see it. They do not consider the viewpoints and feelings of their victims—persons who are treated rudely, whose property is stolen or damaged, or in extreme cases, who are physically injured. Most exercises in this book are intended to increase empathy. However, all "taking another perspective" and "visualization" chapters aim specifically at helping children and youth to have empathy.

Objectives

To give children practice empathizing—imagining others' thoughts, feelings, and perceptions—when others are treated dishonestly or honestly. To help children understand that dishonest persons do NOT have empathy for their victims.

Time Required

Variable. The exercises are brief, guided discussion episodes. A particular scenario may elicit just a few answers, or may stimulate more extensive ideas and relevant personal experiences about thoughts, feelings, and perceptions.

Getting Started

Try to help children become "empathy conscious." Discuss up front the EXTREME importance (to our values) of looking at things from other people's viewpoints. Emphasize that "Because our values and interests are different, different people will see the same thing in quite different ways." For example, "A person being robbed sees the situation much differently than the robber does"; "A person who is cheated or treated rudely sees things much differently than does the person doing the cheating or being rude."

Emphasize that "People often treat others badly because they look at things differently. They do not look at their hurtful behavior from the victim's point of view. They do not think about the victim's feelings. They do not think about the victims right to honest and friendly treatment."

Explain that "This activity will give us some practice looking at things from other people's points of view. We will 'get into their shoes.' We will try to understand other people's thoughts and feelings." Encourage children to try hard to "get into the shoes" or "climb into the skin" of the other person to "imagine the other person's thoughts and feelings."

The scenarios are brief. Read or paraphrase the scenario and then ask for the thoughts, feelings, and perceptions of the different people in the situation.

Follow-Up

Each exercise includes its own follow-up suggestions. The important point is to help children imagine the thoughts, feelings, and perceptions of each person involved—particularly the victim, but sometimes the perpetrator or others. This helps clarify the impact on victims and the thoughtless lack of empathy of the perpetrator.

The parent or teacher might be ready with some actual examples of misbehavior, related to the particular episode, in which the feelings and rights of the victim were totally ignored. These should not be difficult to find, particularly if local news reports include vandalism and "big city" types of beatings, robberies, assaults, rapes, child abuse, drug deals, and murders. The empathy-conscious parent or teacher might maintain a collection of hurtful and delinquent behavior and crimes (e.g., news articles) to use in discussions of lack of empathy and lack of respect for others' rights.

The parent or teacher can remind children how different people's values and interests lead them to see things quite differently than "you or I" might see the same thing.

Some impromptu "What would happen if . . . ?" questions can reinforce the kinds of empathy and perspective-taking of the present problems. For example, "What would happen if none of us ever considered anyone else's feelings in this classroom (or family)?", "What would happen if everyone vandalized or stole each others' property without considering others' rights and feelings?", "What would happen if nobody ever considered the feelings of elderly people who are ignored or treated badly?"

Taking Other Perspectives: Honesty

Scenario 11.1.	**You Are Cheated**

Imagine you are cheated. Imagine that another child, Chuck the Cheater, sells you a boom box for $15. But you later discover that it's broken. It doesn't work. It's a piece of junk!

How do you feel?

What do you think about this?

Is it fun to be cheated this way?

Did Chuck the Cheater consider your feelings?

Did Chuck think about your rights?

Why didn't he think about your rights and feelings?

Scenario 11.2.	**Dayvene's Watch Is Stolen**

Imagine that Dayvene's mother gave her a new digital watch for her birthday. She loved her new watch and did not want to scratch it. So she put it in her locker—and somebody stole it!

How does the Dayvene feel?

What does Dayvene think about after this happens? What ideas go through her head?

What will Dayvene's mother think?

How will she feel?

Was the thief thinking of Dayvene's feelings? Why not?

Was the thief only thinking of himself or herself? Is this right?

Scenario 11.3. **Robert Steals a Sweater**

Imagine that a teenager, Robert, enters a small shop and steals an expensive sweater. He stuffs in his back pack when nobody is looking and walks out of the store.

What does the shop owner think when he or she discovers that the sweater has been stolen?

How does the shop owner feel?

What are Robert's thoughts or feelings?

Did Robert consider the shop owner's point of view

Imagine now that the shop owner calls the police and Robert is caught!

What are Robert's feelings now?

Does he realize he made a mistake?

How do Robert's parents feel when the police explain what Robert did? Are they proud of Robert? Are they embarrassed? Ashamed? Angry?

Scenario 11.4. **Vandalizing a Car**

Late at night a three teenagers, two boys and a girl, see a nice expensive car on a dark street. They break the headlights, smash a couple of windows, tear off the windshield wipers and the side mirrors, bend the radio antenna, and scratch the paint with a big nail. The next morning the car owner, a young nurse, finds her car.

How does she feel?

What does she think?

What were the thoughts of the vandals—why did they do that?

Did they consider the nurse's point of view or her feelings? Why not?

Scenario 11.5. **Not Returning a Calculator**

Imagine Steve loaned his new pocket calculator to Jenny—who never returned it. She kept telling Steve, "Oh, maybe tomorrow."

How does Steve feel?

What are Steve's thoughts?

What does Steve think of Jenny?

What do you think of Jenny? Is she an honest, trustworthy person?

What does Steve think about loaning things now?

What were Jenny's thoughts? Did she consider Steve's feelings?

Did Jenny have the right to keep Steve's calculator? Why not?

Scenario 11.6.   **You Are a Dishonest Creep!**

Imagine that you are a lying, cheating, stealing, dishonest creep. You lie to everyone about everything. You cheat in games. You steal everything that is not nailed down. And everyone knows that you are dishonest and untrustworthy.

How does it feel to be a dishonest, untrustworthy creep?

Do people respect you and think you are a wonderful person?

Would people want you for a friend?

Do YOU like who you are?

Do YOU have self-respect?

Scenario 11.7.   **Keeping a Promise**

Imagine that you promised—absolutely—to take a neighbor boy with you to an adventure movie that he really wanted to see. But you forgot your promise and went without him.

How does the neighbor boy feel?

What does he think of you? Does he trust you?

How would you feel if you really did this?

Are keeping promises and being trustworthy important?

Scenario 11.8.   **Cheating on a Test**

Imagine that Chris cheated on an important test. Before the test, Chris was in the classroom alone. The teacher had gone to the office, Chris saw the test on the teacher's desk, and copied the answers. The next day, Chris got a perfect score. The teacher wrote "A+" and "Excellent Work!" on the test. The teacher also announced to the class that "Chris studied very hard and got a perfect score!"

How does Chris feel? Is Chris proud of the perfect test score? Why not?

Imagine now that someone had looked in the window, saw Chris copying the answers, and mentioned this to the teacher. Instead of finding an "A+" on the paper, Chris finds a note that says, "I believe you cheated on this test. Please see me after school."

Now how does Chris feel? Proud? Happy about cheating?

Is cheating a good idea?

Does it make you feel proud when you cheat?

Scenario 11.9. **Fibbing to Mom**

Imagine that you accidentally bumped your mom's car with your bike and left a small dent and scratch. When she asks if you know how it happened, you say "I don't know anything it about it. I wasn't near the car."

Will your mom trust you more if she finds that you lied to her?

Would it be better to say, "I'm sorry. I bumped it with my bike. I didn't mean to do it. I'll be more careful. Sorry."

Scenario 11.10. **Dog Gone—and Returned**

Imagine that you have a wonderful new pet—a collie dog that you named *Lady*. A week after you got her, Lady wanders off and is lost. Your mom puts an ad in the newspaper's Lost and Found column, and a boy your age shows up at your door with Lady—all safe and sound! He says, "Here is your dog. I knew you would be sad without her!"

How do you feel?

Are you glad the boy thought about your feelings?

Should we try to understand other people's problems and feelings?

Chapter

12

Visualization:
More Empathy About
Honesty and Trustworthiness

Visualization Exercises

Visualization exercises continue the effort to help children empathize. Children relax, shut their eyes, and visualize a scenario that describes some mistreatment, injustice, or other hurtful (or perhaps pleasant and helpful) behavior. As with Taking Another Perspective, children are asked to imagine the thoughts, feelings, and perceptions of the people involved. Some narrations are humorous; some are not amusing at all.

Creative challenge: If there is an important value or attitude that you would like to emphasize but is not covered in the scenarios in this book, try writing your own script. It may be easier than you think. You can have children imagine the feelings of someone treated either dishonestly or with honesty and respect for his or her feelings and rights.

Time Required

The introductions and narrations require about 10 minutes. The follow-up clarifications of feelings and perceptions should require another 10 minutes.

Getting Started

Explain the importance of understanding other people's feelings and other people's points of view. Remind children that "We are less likely to carelessly hurt or mistreat others if we think about what it is like to be hurt or mistreated. This exercise will help us see things from other people's points of view, and help us understand how other people feel when they are treated badly. The exercise also will help us understand how bad we look to others when we behave poorly."

Explain that everyone is to "get comfortable, shut your eyes, and let your imagination come alive as I tell the story." Read or paraphrase the scenarios clearly and moderately slowly, with pauses where indicated by ellipses (. . .).

Follow-Up

Each scenario includes its own discussion questions. After each scenario, ask children—in their role as victim or observer of bad behavior—to describe their thoughts, feelings, and perceptions. Be sure to clarify these so that all children understand the views and feelings of the persons in the scenarios. As with follow-ups to other exercises, try to have children agree that "This behavior is bad. It hurts other people. It hurts yourself. We should not do this, should we."

A problem solving approach also may help clarify the values lessons of the visualization exercises. The two-step procedure can help children (1) understand why the situation is a problem ("What is the problem?"), and (2) itemize some solutions ("How can we solve it?"). A problem solving approach focuses directly on what should or should not be done.

Visualizing Honesty and Dishonesty

Scenario 12.1.   You Are Very Old

Imagine that you are a very old person . . . You live alone in a little apartment . . . As you have grown older you have become smaller and weaker . . . Can you feel how weak you are? . . . Your family lives very far away, and cannot visit you or help you . . . You have very little money, barely enough to pay rent and buy groceries . . . How do you feel? . . . Do you feel safe and secure? . . . Do you feel worried? . . . Do you feel you are in good control of your life? . . . Are you lonely? . . .

Today is the day you expect your Social Security check to come in the mail . . . It's your only money . . . You hear your mailman in the apartment hallway, and you hear him leave . . . In a few minutes you put on a sweater and you open the door to go to your mailbox . . . You see two teenagers at the mailboxes . . . They are much bigger and stronger than you are . . . They are prying open mailboxes and stealing everyone's checks . . . They have just taken yours and turn and laugh at you . . . "Thanks for the check!" they yell as they run out the door . . . Now you cannot pay the rent . . . You cannot buy groceries . . . You cannot give your friend next door a birthday present . . .

How do you feel?

Is it right for someone like you to have your money stolen?

Why would anyone do this to you?

Why would young people steal from the elderly?

Do they think about the feelings and problems of the elderly?

Do they think about your rights?

Scenario 12.2.   Your Home Is Vandalized

Imagine you have just returned home from the grocery store with your mother . . . You walk into the kitchen and discover that your home has been vandalized . . . Drawers are pulled open and dumped on the floor . . . The refrigerator is open and everything spilled all over . . . Smashed eggs are dripping down the wall . . . There also are big gouges and cuts in the wall . . . Then you discover that some things have been stolen . . . The radio your mother got for her birthday is gone . . . The new microwave oven is gone . . . Even the telephone and the electric mixer are gone . . . You enter the living room, and the TV is missing . . . The new hi-fi set and the speakers are gone . . . Your newest cassettes are gone . . . Your camera is gone from the table where you left it . . . All of the pictures from the walls are smashed on the floor . . . Your mom's knick-knacks from the shelves are on the floor, most are broken . . . One lamp is smashed, the other one is gone . . .

How do you feel?

How does your mother feel?

Is it enjoyable to have things that are important to you destroyed or stolen?

Is it fair for someone to do this to you and your family?

Why would anyone do this to you and your family?

Did they think about your feelings and rights?

Scenario 12.3.   Kate's Broken Promises[1]

You are waiting for your friend Kate in front of the school . . . The time is 3:45 p.m. Kate promised to be there (for sure!) at 3:30 . . . You are not surprised she's late, because Kate forgets her promises all the time . . . Today she was supposed to return your cassettes . . . You wonder if you will ever see them again, because Kate doesn't return things very well either . . . Finally, you give up and go home . . . At eight o'clock that evening Kate calls and asks, "Can I borrow your calculator for a class project?" . . . You hesitate, then say, "Sure, I'll bring it to school tomorrow." Then you ask, "Where were you today, Kate? I waited for you for half an hour." . . . "Well, I went to the hobby store with Fred for some colored paper. Meet me tomorrow at 3:30—I promise I'll be there . . . Oh, I had a little problem with one of your cassettes. It fell in some mud, but I think it still sounds all right, sort of . . . It wasn't my fault" . . . "Sure Kate," you say. "That's okay. I'll see you tomorrow" . . .

Should Kate have met you when she said she would? Why?

Is it important to keep promises? Why?

Is it all right to keep people waiting like Kate did? Why?

How do you feel when people don't return your things, or else they return them broken?

Why is it important to return things promptly and in good condition?

How do you really feel about your friend Kate? Is she trustworthy?

Did Kate think about your feelings? Your rights?

Would you like a lot of friends like Kate?

Should YOU be like Kate?

Scenario 12.4.   Leroy Joins a Gang

Leroy is in high school and is a good student . . . Imagine that Leroy's friends talked him into joining their gang, the "Gangster Gang" . . . They showed Leroy the great "Wendover Wildcats" jackets that they all wore . . . Nobody else would DARE wear those jackets . . . They told Leroy that the Gangster Gang is cool, and they not afraid of anybody because they protect each other . . . They told him about gang signs and

---

[1]This visualization exercise also appears in *Values Are Forever*.

gang colors and how to wear his Wendover Wildcats baseball hat . . .
They told him he could make money selling drugs . . . and maybe
robbing stores . . . They told him he would have to drop out of school—
which is "too much work and a lot of crap anyway" . . . They told him
they all had guns, and that "If anybody gives US trouble, we'll blow 'em
away!" . . . They did not tell Leroy that some gang members were in jail
for selling drugs . . . None of them could get a job . . . and one member
and his girl friend were in the hospital with bullet wounds . . . They had
been shot by members of the "Crooked Criminals" gang . . . So Leroy
joined the Gangster Gang.

> Is Leroy proud of to be a member of the Gangster Gang? Is he proud
> of his new jacket?
>
> Does Leroy think about what could happen to him?
>
> Leroy's mother knows all about gang violence and crime. What do
> you suppose SHE thinks of the Gangster Gang?
>
> Is she glad Leroy joined the Gangster gang?
>
> Is she proud of Leroy?
>
> Is she worried about Leroy?
>
> What do you think of the Gangster Gang's values: Drugs, robbery,
> carrying guns, and being ready to shoot somebody over almost
> nothing?

Scenario 12.5.   The End of Raymond and Leroy

Raymond is 17 years old . . . He is a new member of the Crooked
Criminals gang . . . One day, Raymond was walking down the street
wearing his gang jacket, an Oakland Bears jacket . . . He saw Leroy
wearing a Wendover Wildcats gang jacket. Raymond flashed the Crooked
Criminals gang sign . . . Leroy flashed the Gangster Gang sign . . .
Raymond did what his friends said to do, he pulled out his gun and shot
Leroy twice in the stomach . . . Leroy died in the hospital two hours later.

> Was joining the Gangster Gang a good decision or a bad decision for
> Leroy?
>
> How does Leroy's mother feel?
>
> How does the rest of Leroy's family feel? Are they happy? Are they
> proud he was a member of the Gangster Gang?
>
> Did Raymond, the boy who shot Leroy, think about Leroy's feelings
> or rights?

What was Raymond thinking when he shot Leroy? Why did he do it? Is that an intelligent reason to kill someone?

Imagine that Raymond was arrested, convicted of murder, and sent to prison for 30 years.

Is Raymond happy he killed Leroy?

Will Raymond enjoy living in a cage and not having any freedom?

Is Raymond's mother glad that her son was a "Crooked Criminals" gang member? How does she feel?

Did Leroy and Raymond both makes BIG mistakes with their lives? How?

Do gangs have good values or destructive values?

Would YOU make the same mistakes Leroy and Raymond made?

Scenario 12.5. **You Are Honest and Trustworthy**

Imagine that you have always been an honest, trustworthy, dependable person . . . You enjoy being fair in games . . . keeping promises . . . never stealing anything . . . returning things that you borrow . . . being on time and doing what people expect you to do . . . Your neighbors know about your habit of being honest and trustworthy . . . They hire you to care for their pets and water their plants when they are on vacation . . . They hire you to do yard work . . . They tell you, "I like the way you work . . . you are so honest and dependable" . . .

Do you feel good about being an honest, trustworthy person?

Is your mom proud of you?

Should everyone be honest, trustworthy, and dependable?

13

Questions and Discussion About Cheating, Stealing, and Other Virtues

Because it is such a common teaching technique, using questions to stimulate thought and discussion may be the most familiar teaching strategy in this book.

Objectives

As with the other activities in this section, the goals are to:

- Raise awareness about and clarify *honesty* as a values and behavior problem.

- Help children understand why honesty is better than dishonesty in regard to its effects on others and themselves.

- Help children clarify their own feelings and identities regarding honesty.

- Help children empathize with people who are victimized by theft or other forms of dishonesty.

- Help children understand that they will feel better about themselves, have more self-respect, and earn the respect of others if they decide to be "honest persons."

■ Most importantly, help children make conscious commitments to being honest and trustworthy.

Time Required

Totally flexible; use whatever time is comfortable. If an issue is simple and clear, a few minutes (even seconds) may adequately cover a particular values question. Ten to 20 minutes might be spent on sets of related questions. More time would be needed if the teacher or parent slips in an appropriate brainstorming or "What would happen if . . . ?" problem.

Getting Started

Little is needed beyond an introduction that orients children to the purpose and content of the discussion. For example, you might explain that "We're going to think about honesty, how we have been hurt by dishonest people, and what kind of person you would like to be."

Discussion Questions About Honesty

GENERAL

13.1   What is an honest, trustworthy person? What is an honest, trustworthy person like?

13.2   Does an honest, trustworthy person respect himself or herself? Does an honest, trustworthy person have a lot of self-respect?

13.3   It is important for us to like who we are? To respect ourselves?

13.4   Do other people respect someone who is honest? Is it important for others to respect us?

13.5   Would you want to be a person whom nobody can trust?

13.6   Does an honest person think about other people's feelings? Is it important to think about other people's feelings? Why?

13.7   Can we do this? Can we try to take the role of a person who has been cheated or whose things have been stolen? Can we climb right inside their skin and try to understand how they feel?

13.8   What if somebody's bicycle or new roller blades were stolen? Can we understand how they feel? Should we look at the problem from their point of view?

13.9   Some people make our neighborhoods better and some people make our neighborhoods worse. Do people who steal things make a neighborhood better or worse? Do we respect them?

13.10   Some people vandalize—they destroy property, spray paint walls and bus stops, damage cars, and break school windows. Do these people make a neighborhood better or worse?

13.11   Which kind of person are you? Are you the kind of person who makes a neighborhood better? Or are you the kind of person who makes a neighborhood worse?

CHEATING

13.12   What is cheating? What are some different kinds of cheating?

13.13   What's wrong with cheating?

13.14   Is it all right to cheat if we don't get caught?

13.15   How do you feel when you have been cheated?

13.16   What do you think of the person who cheated you?

13.17   What kind of people cheat—maybe they sell you something that is no good, or they cheat at games, or they cheat on tests at school?

13.18   Are they honest, trustworthy people? Do we respect people who cheat?

STEALING

13.19   What is wrong with stealing?

13.20   Should everyone steal? Why not?

13.21   How do you feel when something of yours is stolen?

13.22   What do you think of the person who stole it?

13.23   Are people who steal honest, trustworthy people?

13.24   Do we respect people who steal?

VANDALISM

13.25   What is vandalism?

13.26   Have you ever had anything vandalized?

13.27   How did you feel?

13.28   What did you think of the person who did this to you?

13.29   What kind of people vandalize? Are they intelligent, thoughtful, considerate, honest people?

13.30   Do we respect people who vandalize?

LYING

13.31   What about lying? Is it okay to tell lies? What about "little white lies" (like "I just love your new pet snake!")?

13.32   Do you respect yourself when you have to lie to keep out of trouble?

13.33.   Do you feel guilty when you tell a lie? Do you feel bad about yourself? Maybe kind of rotten?

13.34   Do you lose a little self-respect when you tell lies?

13.35   Will others like you, respect you, and trust you when they find out that you lied to them?

13.36   How do you feel when you learn that someone lied to you? (Maybe they said they had to do homework because they didn't feel like talking to you on the phone.)

13.37   What do you think of people who lie to you?

13.38   What kind of people have to tell lies? (People who are trying to hide something?)

13.39   Is that the kind of person you want to be?

NOT RETURNING THINGS

13.40   Is it all right to borrow things?

13.41   Is it all right NOT to return the things that you borrow?

13.42   Is this like stealing?

13.43   How do you feel when you loan something and the person does not return it?

13.44   What do you think of people who do not return things they borrow?

13.45   Are you the kind of person who returns things when you promise to return them?

KEEPING PROMISES

13.46   Is breaking promises a kind of dishonesty? Why?

13.47   Is it best to keep promises that you make?

13.48   What do you think of someone who does not keep his or her promises? Are they Honest? Trustworthy?

13.49   Do you respect people who do not keep their promises?

13.50   Are you the kind of person who keeps promises?

14

Word Search and Crossword Puzzles About Honesty

The next pages present one word search and one crossword puzzle about honesty. Nearly all kids know all about word search puzzles and most understand crosswords, but instructions are presented anyway. The puzzles are on separate pages so a teacher may copy and distribute them to the class, or a parent may copy them so his or her kids need not write in the book. The solutions are at the end of this chapter.

Word Search: Honesty Words

You probably have done work search puzzles.

Words related to HONESTY are hidden in the block of letters.

The words are printed left to right or top to bottom. One word is printed backwards—right to left.

Find these words and draw a ring around them.

Cheat	Helpful	Hurtful
Honest	Lie	Steal
Truth	Vandalism	Trustworthy

```
H  O  N  E  S  T  M
J  H  C  Q  X  R  W
V  E  M  V  U  U  Z
A  L  Q  C  D  S  A
N  P  T  R  U  T  H
D  F  Y  F  S  W  U
A  U  L  X  T  O  R
L  L  B  Z  E  R  T
I  C  H  E  A  T  F
S  G  N  W  L  H  U
M  E  I  L  K  Y  L
```

From *Teaching Values* published by Westwood Publishing Co. © 1996 Gary A. Davis

Crossword Puzzle: Honesty, Trustworthiness

Have you ever worked a crossword puzzle?

They are fun—and challenging!

Write the answers or ideas in the "checkerboard," with one letter in each little square. Start each answer in the square that has the same number as the question.

Most of the words are related to honesty. But some are not.

Write "Across" words in the regular way, from left to right.

Write "Down" words from top to bottom (vertically).

From *Teaching Values* published by Westwood Publishing Co. © 1996 Gary A. Davis

ACROSS

2. Dishonesty hurts ourselves and hurts _____.

6. This puzzle is about being _____.

8. Opposite of *off*.

10. Initials of Utah State University.

11. A very proper way to address a gentleman. (Rhymes with *stir*.)

12. Instead of *buying* things, some dishonest young people try to _____.

14. Nickname for a funny person. (Squirrel food).

DOWN

1. Trustworthy people keep their _____.

3. Edward's nickname.

4. Not a daughter.

5. When we borrow things, we must _____ them.

7. If your friends are honest, you can _____ them.

9. We don't like it when people _____ in games by not following the rules.

13. When somebody says something that is not true, they are telling a _____.

15. Opposite of "them."

Solutions to Puzzles

Word Search

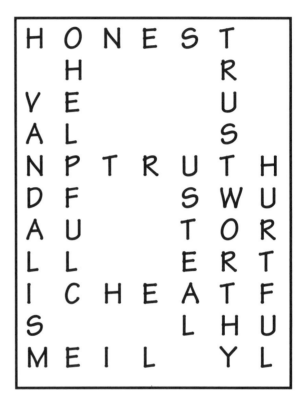

Crossword Puzzle

A Quiz About Helpful and Hurtful Values

Directions to children and youth

"Helpful" values help others and ourselves.

"Hurtful" values hurt others and ourselves.

Let's see if you can tell which are "helpful" values and which are "hurtful" values.

Let's take a quiz.

For each question, check "Good Value" if the action

✓ HELPS other people.

✓ HELPS yourself.

✓ HELPS you respect yourself.

✓ HELPS others to respect you. Causes them to think you are a pleasant and trustworthy person.

Check "Bad Value" if the action

✓ HURTS other people.

✓ HURTS you, your self-respect, your future, or your health.

✓ Causes others to lose respect for you. Causes them to think you are NOT a very pleasant or trustworthy person.

A VALUES QUIZ

	Good Value	Bad Value
1. You will be a teenager soon, and it's time to act "grown up"—and start smoking.	☐	☐
2. You decide it's best to be fair. You take turns in games. You share things. You let everyone help decide what to do.	☐	☐
3. When you use the school restrooms, you draw and scribble on the walls. You toss waste paper on the floor. You know the custodian will have to clean up your mess.	☐	☐
4. Imagine you live in North Dakota. It just snowed 8 inches. Your 80-year-old neighbor is starting to shovel her sidewalk. You shovel it for her, because you believe in helpfulness.	☐	☐
5. You shovel it for her because you also respect elderly people (and you can imagine what it is like to be older and weaker).	☐	☐
6. You shovel it for her because you know you will feel REAL good about helping someone in need. You will be proud of yourself.	☐	☐

	Good Value	Bad Value
7. You don't care about your elderly neighbor and her problems. You don't care what she thinks of you. So you tell her you will shovel her walk if she will pay you $5.	☐	☐
8. You ignore your neighbor and her snow, because you need to think about YOURSELF—you need to watch TV or phone somebody. (Her snow isn't your problem!)	☐	☐
9. When you go into drugstores, you mess up the magazine rack. When you go into department stores you mess up the neat stacks of clothes. The clerks have to clean up your messes, but you don't care.	☐	☐
10. Imagine you are 16 and riding in a car with friends. You just finished your Big Mac, with a soda. You pitch your wrappers and drink cup out the car window.	☐	☐
11. You are at your friend Pat's house. You see a cassette tape of your favorite rock group. When Pat isn't looking, you stick it in your your pocket. You say "Well, gotta' go now."	☐	☐

	Good Value	Bad Value
12. Actually, you value friends and you value being trustworthy. You don't steal anything. You help Pat with some math problems. Then you buy Pat an ice cream cone at McDonald's.	☐	☐
13. When you are at McDonald's, you and Pat yell at each other across the restaurant. You use really bad swear words, so that the elderly people will know that you don't care about their rights.	☐	☐
14. Actually, you respect the elderly. You smile and say "Hello" to them. You hold the door open for them. They smile and say "Thank you." They think you are a nice person.	☐	☐
15. You think way, way ahead about your life. You do not want to spend it in jail. You do not want to be on welfare. You want to have a good job or career. You know you must complete high school. Then you want to go to a technical college or a university.	☐	☐
16. You think way, way ahead about WHO and WHAT you want to be when you grow up—a successful and happy person who is able to earn money and enjoy life.	☐	☐

There ARE right and wrong answers to these values questions.

How are your values?

Do you care about other people's feelings?

Do you want to be fair to others?

Do you value self-respect and respect from others?

Are you thinking about "What kind of human being am I?"

Part IV

Our Rights and Others' Rights

16

About Our Rights and Others' Rights:

A "Values Bill of Rights"

Understanding Others' Rights, Our Rights

In Chapter 1 we noted that a core idea in this book is helping young people understand that "We have no right to mistreat others" and that "Others have no right to mistreat us." The word *rights* appears throughout this book. If *rights* needs to be explained to children, consider the following:

When we say "You have rights," it means that *you deserve to be treated fairly, honestly, and nicely*. That's all. Rights are very important. Everyone has rights.

Your parents (and step-parents) have rights.

Your brothers and sisters (and step-brothers and step-sisters) have rights.

Your teachers, neighbors, store clerks, bus drivers, and school custodians have rights, too.

Everyone has rights, even people we don't know.

"Respecting others' rights" just means treating people fairly, honestly, and nicely. "Respecting others' rights" means treating people the way YOU like to be treated.

Even your pets have rights—your dog, cat, canary, goldfish, gerbil, and toad! They have a right to be cared for and not mistreated.

After your rights discussion, you might probe for understanding with "Do you understand what rights are?" "Should people respect our rights?" "Is respecting other people's rights a good idea? Yes? No? Maybe?" "We do not want our rights violated, so it is wrong to violate others' rights. Does that make sense?

The next page contains a miniature rights poster.[1] If you wish, you are welcome to make a transparency, post a copy on the wall, give each child a copy, or as an art project have children make a full-size copy.

---

[1] Available in 18" × 24" size from Westwood Publishing Company, Box 222, Cross Plains, WI 53528, as part of a set of five different values posters.

VALUES BILL OF RIGHTS

No one has the "right" . . .

> to hurt you.
>
> to steal your things.
>
> to damage your things.
>
> to be unfair to you, to cheat you, to lie to you.
>
> to leave messes—for you or others to clean up.
>
> to be rude to you.
>
> to be cruel to you.
>
> to shove or punch smaller children because they feel like it.
>
> to touch you where you don't want to be touched.

YOU do not have the "right" . . .

> to steal someone's things just because you want them.
>
> to damage other people's things.
>
> to be unfair to others or to cheat them.
>
> to make others clean up your messes.
>
> to be mean or rude to others.
>
> to shove or punch little kids because you feel like it.
>
> to touch others where they do not want to be touched.
>
> to snoop through your friends' things, your sister's things, or your parent's things.

YOU, YOUR FRIENDS, YOUR TEACHER, AND OTHERS . . .

> have the "right" to be treated fairly, honestly, and nicely.

Chapter

17

"What Would Happen If ...

Nobody Ever Helped Anyone?"

_____

Objectives

As we noted in Chapters 4 and 7, many young people do not think about the consequences of their actions, actions that often violate others' rights to fair and cordial treatment. Some actions violate others' right to live. The purpose of these "What would happen if . . . ?" exercises is to raise awareness of others rights and our rights. As in all activities of this book, central goals are logical understanding, empathy, and eliciting commitments to respecting others' rights.

Time Required

Each "What would happen if . . . ?" exercise should require about 3 to 10 minutes, depending on the particular problem and children's interest. Introductions and follow-ups add to the time requirement.

Getting Started

Discuss the meaning of "respecting others' rights," perhaps as sketched in Chapter 16, with emphasis on our rights and the rights of others to be treated fairly, honestly, and nicely.

Explain that "We are going to think about what happens as a result of violating others' rights. We are going to think about other people's feelings and our feelings."

Explain that "The problem will begin with 'What would happen if . . . ?' and you can use your imaginations to think about what happens when people violate our rights in different ways."

Follow-Up

Each activity includes its own follow-up, thought-prodding questions. As always, try to stimulate empathy and commitment.

"What Would Happen If . . . ?" Problems About Respecting Others' Rights

---

Problem 17.1 **What would happen if we decided that nobody has the right to be treated in a friendly way?** It's just fine to be rude and nasty to everybody we talk to—parents, brothers and sisters, neighbors, other kids in the neighborhood and at school, teachers, principals, store clerks, bus drivers, custodians—everybody. What would happen?

> Would we be happier?
>
> Would anybody like us?
>
> Would we have any friends?
>
> Do we have a right to be treated in a friendly way?
>
> Is it better to be treated in a friendly way?

Problem 17.2 People are different, aren't they. We come in different sizes, shapes and colors. **What would happen if everybody decided to be rude, unpleasant, and even cruel to anybody who wasn't exactly like they were?** Anybody who is a little bit different gets insulted, ignored, teased, criticized, and called names. What would happen?

> Is this fair? Why not?
>
> Do we all have a right to be treated fairly and nicely?

Problem 17.3 **What would happen if nobody were friendly to YOU?** How would you feel?

> Would you feel happy? Sad?
>
> Do you like to be treated in friendly ways?
>
> Which is best, being friendly or unfriendly?

Problem 17.4   **What would happen if nobody ever helped their mom (dad, care giver) around the house or apartment?** Everybody leaves their coats, sweaters and dirty clothes lying around. Nobody helps with dishes or cleaning up after meals. Everybody leaves messes in the kitchen, the bathroom, their bedrooms, and the room with the TV.

Is it fair to make someone else clean up all the messes and do all the work around the house (or apartment)?

Does mom have a right to some help once in a while?

If you were mom, would you like some help?

Problem 17.5   Pretend you ARE your mom. **What would happen if your child was very helpful?** If he or she helped with dishes and tried not to leave messes for you to clean up? What would happen?

Would you feel good?

Would you appreciate the help?

Would you think you have a fine, thoughtful child who respects your rights?

Problem 17.6   Imagine that Bully Bob is bigger than most people in the school. And Bully Bob has a bad attitude. **What would happen if Bully Bob were in the habit of pushing everybody around and punching people whenever he felt like it?**

Does Bully Bob have the right to push smaller kids around and punch them whenever he feels like it?

Do you like to be pushed around and punched?

What do you think of people like Bully Bob?

Should Bully Bob respect people's right to be treated nicely?

Problem 17.7   **What would happen if nobody ever helped anybody else?** If you need help with your homework, that's too bad—nobody is going to help you. If the elderly lady next door needs help carrying groceries or shoveling snow, that's too bad for her. If a blind or disabled lady trips and falls in the street, we all just step over her.

Would everyone be happier and better off if nobody ever helped anybody with anything?

Is it fair not to help people who need help?

Do people have a right to be helped?

If we needed help with something (maybe homework or lifting something heavy), would we be happy if somebody helped us?

Does it make us feel good to help people?

Problem 17.8   **What would happen if all the children in this school (neighborhood) decided to steal everything they could get their hands on?** Everybody believes that they have a right to steal your things. What would happen?

Does anyone have a right to steal your things?

Do you like your things stolen?

Do you have a right to your own property?

Is it right to steal people's things?

Problem 17.9   **What would happen if everybody decided that breaking people's things and vandalizing public property is a lot of fun and a good thing to do?** Some kids trash bicycles in the bike rack. Some kids break anything they see in desks or lockers. Some kids damage hallways and rest rooms. Some kids spray paint the bus stop and the bus. Some kids break school windows, car windows, and building windows at night. What would happen if everyone were vandals, if everyone did this sort of thing?

Does anyone have the right to destroy other people's property?

What about public property?

Is something better or more beautiful when it is broken or spray painted?

Do you like your things broken or destroyed by others?

Should we be vandals and destroy people's things and public property?

Problem 17.10   **What would happen if everybody always made big-time messes in every store and restaurant?** In grocery stores and drug stores people mess up shelves and knock things on the floor. In department stores they trash all the displays and put things back in the wrong places. In restaurants they make messes on the table, the chairs, and the floor—messes for somebody else to clean up.

Do we have the right to leave messes for others to clean up?

Is it fair to people who work in stores or restaurants for us to leave extra big messes?

Do people who work in stores and restaurants have any rights?

Do they have a right to expect us NOT to make extra work for them?

If you were a store clerk or a waiter or waitress, how would you feel if everybody always left huge messes for you to straighten up?

Brainstorming About Rights:

"What Rights Do Children Have?"

Objectives

To foster understanding of our rights and others' rights, and to help children make commitments to respecting the rights of others.

Time Required

From 3 to 8 minutes per problem, depending upon the problem, children's interest, and whether or not it is Friday afternoon. You probably will want to work on several related problems in each thinking session.

If children run out of ideas, ask "Anyone else have an idea?" Solicit ideas from quieter children: "Latricia, do you have an idea or two?" You also can contribute ideas.

Getting Started

Introduce or review the meaning of "rights" and "respecting others' rights," perhaps by asking children "What do we mean by 'rights'?" or "What do we mean by 'violating others' rights'?"

Explain that we are going to think about our rights and others' rights by using brainstorming.

Review brainstorming rules:

✓ We will think of all the ideas we can; we want a long list of ideas.

✓ We won't criticize each other's ideas, because criticism is like punishment.

You may paraphrase the problems.

A teacher may use a large- or small-group format. For variety, you can brainstorm a problem (or two) with the entire class, then break into small groups for an additional problem (or two). Each small group would report all of its ideas, or just its best ideas, to the class.

Guiding The Session

Additional ideas for many problems can be stimulated if the teacher (or parent) suggests contexts: In school, at home, as a neighbor, at friends' homes, on the playground, in shopping malls, in movie theaters, when playing games, in parks or picnic places, or on the sidewalks and streets.

In addition to contexts, with broad problems (such as 18.1) the teacher (or parent) can suggest categories that involve rights, such as how people *talk* to us (rudely, with bad language, snobbishly, in threatening ways); whether people treat us *honestly and fairly* (or steal and cheat); and whether people *play fair* in games and share (or cheat or are greedy). *Vandalizing, damaging our property, leaving messes,* and *not helping* also are categories that might stimulate ideas about rights.

In the event that children draw a total blank, many of the brainstorming problems include answers that a teacher or parent may suggest.

Follow-Up

With any of these problems, follow-up discussion can focus on children's personal examples of violations of their rights and violations of others' rights. They undoubtedly will have many.

Have people treated us rudely? Yelled at us for no reason? When? ("When?" means "please explain—how, when, etc.")

Have people stolen our things? When?

Have people deliberately damaged our things or other people's things or public property? When?

Have people been unpleasant with your family or other relatives? When?

Have people cheated you, your family, or other relatives? When?

With problem 18.1, "What rights do we ALL have," the teacher or parent can ask:

Does it make any difference WHO we are?

Does it make any difference if we are Hawaiian, African American, Hispanic, Asian, white, Native American, or from India or Egypt?

Do we all have a right to fair, honest, friendly treatment?"

There are many possible commitment-provoking follow-up questions, such as:

How do we feel when people are rude and unpleasant to us? When our right to pleasant treatment is violated? Are we really pleased?

Should we be rude and unpleasant to other children? To our parents? To neighbors? Should we be rude and unpleasant to anybody?

How do we feel when our things are stolen? Are we happy? Do people have a right to steal our things?

Should we steal other people's things?

How do we feel when other people deliberately damage our things? Does this make us happy? Do people have a right to damage our things?

Should we damage other people's things? Should we tear their books, break their pencils, kick their bicycles, ruin their cassette tapes, . . . ?

Are you the kind of person who will try to respect other people's rights?

And don't forget, the teacher or parent can use "What would happen if . . . ?", brainstorming, problem solving ("What is the problem?" and "How can we solve it?"), or any of the other strategies to create original, on-target, and thought-provoking values exercises.

Brainstorming About Our Rights, Others' Rights

Problem 18.1	What rights do ALL of us have—children, parents, teachers, store clerks, and everyone else? Think of all the ideas you can.
Problem 18.2	What rights do children have at home? (To be loved, cared for, listened to, treated with respect, . . .)
Problem 18.3	What rights do children have at school? (To be treated with respect and dignity; to be treated fairly, equally, and in a friendly way; to be protected, . . .)
Problem 18.4	What rights do children have when they are walking home from school? (To be safe, to be treated nicely, . . .)
Problem 18.5	Imagine that Chao-Lin, from China, is a new student in our class. What rights does Chao-Lin have? (To feel welcome, to be treated with friendliness, to be helped in learning about the school and community, . . .)
Problem 18.6	How can you show Chao-Lin that you respect his rights to friendly treatment and fair treatment? Think of all the ideas you can.
Problem 18.7	How many rights can you think of that parents (step-parents, care givers) have? (To be treated pleasantly, to be helped, to NOT have to worry about you, . . .)
Problem 18.8	How can we show our parents (step-parents, care givers) that we respect their rights to nice treatment and to be helped with some chores?
Problem 18.9	What rights do teachers have? (Do we have any rights? What are they?)
Problem 18.10	What rights do grandparents have? (To be visited, to be talked to nicely and politely, . . .)
Problem 18.11	How can we show grandparents that we respect their rights?
Problem 18.12	How many rights can you think of that our brothers and sisters have? ("If you have no brothers or sisters, pretend that you have one brother and one sister.")
Problem 18.13	What rights to children with disabilities have—children who are blind or partially blind, who are deaf or do not hear well, who are in a wheelchair, or who have an illness or a learning problem? (To learn in school, to be talked to, to be treated in a friendly way, to NOT be insulted or treated cruelly! . . .)

Problem 18.14 How can we show people with disabilities that we respect their rights?

Problem 18.15 How many rights can you think of that elderly people have? (On a bus, as neighbors, . . .)

Problem 18.16 How can we show elderly people in our neighborhood that we respect their rights to pleasant treatment and to receive some help once in a while?

Problem 18.17 What rights do store clerks and McDonald's counter people have? (To pleasantness, to not have to clean up extra big messes, . . .)

Problem 18.18 How can we show store clerks and McDonald's counter people that we respect their rights?

Problem 18.19 What rights do our pet cats, dogs, canaries, guinea pigs, and gold fish have?

Problem 18.20 How can we show our pets that we understand their rights? Should we say, "Hi, Mr. Goldfish! I understand your rights"? What should we do?

Problem 18.21 What rights do we have if we are in a movie theater?

Problem 18.22 What rights do school custodians have?

Problem 18.23 How many ways can you think of to show the custodian(s) that you respect their rights and appreciate their work?

Problem 18.24 What rights do school bus drivers have?

Problem 18.25 What rights do WE have on a school bus or a city bus?

Problem 18.26 What rights do we have regarding friendliness?

Problem 18.27 What rights do we have regarding being treated fairly, honestly, and not being cheated?

Problem 18.28 What rights do we have regarding things that we loan.

Problem 18.29 What rights do we have regarding our personal property.

Problem 18.30 What are everyone's rights regarding snooping?

Reverse Brainstorming About Rights:

"How Can We Violate Each Other's Rights?"

Reverse Brainstorming About Rights

You may recall from Chapters 4 and 9 that Reverse Brainstorming often elicits ideas that reflect what people already are doing. Reverse brainstorming thus can be an eye-opening purge of how children already are violating others' rights.

Objectives

To further clarify the nature of rights—our rights and others' rights to fair, honest, and friendly treatment.

Time Required

Five or 10 minutes.

Getting Started

Explain that "We are going to use Reverse Brainstorming to help us think about our rights and other people's rights to be treated fairly, honestly, and nicely."

Remind children that "With Reverse Brainstorming, we turn the problem around. We think of how to make a situation WORSE. This helps us understand how to make things BETTER. Reverse Brainstorming can help us learn to respect other people's rights, and expect them to respect our rights to fair and friendly treatment. Okay?"

Be sure to record ideas on the chalkboard, or have a student volunteer write them, so they will be available for later discussion.

Some discussion-prodding hints are presented with most individual problems.

Follow-Up

Key follow-up questions are:

> DO we ever do these things?

> SHOULD we ever do these things?

Remind children that "We all have a right to good treatment—to be treated honestly, fairly, and nicely."

Probe for *understanding* with:

> Do you understand what rights are?

> Do we want people to respect our right to be treated fairly and pleasantly?

> Should other people respect our right to be treated fairly and pleasantly?

> Should we respect other people's rights to fair and friendly treatment?

Elicit *empathy* with:

> How do we feel when people are rude and unpleasant to us or yell at us? How do we feel when our right to pleasant treatment is violated? Do we like it a lot?

> How do we feel when our things are damaged or stolen? Does that make us happy? Should we damage or steal other people's things?

> We do not want our rights violated, so it is wrong to violate others' rights, make sense?"

> *Are YOU the kind of person who will violate other people's rights?*

Reverse Brainstorming Problems Regarding Rights

Problem 19.1   How many ways can we think of to violate other people's rights? (By stealing? Being rude? Cheating at games? Leaving messes? Vandalizing and breaking things? Not returning things? Not helping? Being cruel? Threatening other children? Shoving and punching them? Snooping? Loud music or noise? Touching? . . .)

Problem 19.2.   In our classroom, how many ways can we think of to violate other children's rights? (To a classroom that is nice, pleasant, safe, and enjoyable; to concentrate; to learn; . . .)

Problem 19.3   How many ways can we think of to violate a teacher's rights? (To respect, pleasantness, attention, a neat classroom, . . .)

Problem 19.4   How many ways can we think of to violate the rights of people who work in stores or at McDonald's? (To nice treatment, to not have to clean up our big messes), . . .

Problem 19.5   How many ways can you think of to be unfriendly and to hurt the feelings of a new student in class (or in the neighborhood)?

Problem 19.6   How many ways can you think of to hurt your mother's or father's (or care giver's) feelings?

Problem 19.7   How many ways can you think of to make MORE work for your mother (father, care giver)? (Make messes, not help, not run errands, make them nag at you to do school work, . . .)

Problem 19.8   How many ways can you think of to show the school custodian(s) that you are really a thoughtless and crummy person? How can you show that you don't care one bit about his or her (their) rights?

Problem 19.9   You are having a picnic in the city park with some friends. How many ways can you show that you do not respect the rights of other groups of picnickers? (Make noise, play loud music, run through their space, use bad language, leave a mess, . . .)

Problem 19.10   Your picnic has ended, and everyone wants to leave. How many ways can you show the park custodians that you do not care about their rights? How can you make more work for them? (Messes, vandalism to tables and restrooms, stomp flower beds, dig holes in grass . . .)

Problem 19.11   Imagine that all of us live in apartments. (Perhaps you already do.) Some neighbors are elderly. Some neighbors work nights and sleep during the day. How can we show that we have no respect for their right to a peaceful and safe place to live? (Music, yelling, loud TV, stomping, slamming doors, leaving things to trip over in hallway, stealing batteries from smoke alarms, blocking exit doors, . . .)

Analogical Thinking:

"How Is Unfair Treatment Like a Finger in a Light Socket?"

_____

Objectives

To use analogies to help children think about and make decisions regarding their rights and other people's rights.

Time Required

Often just a minute or two, perhaps only a few seconds. Be ready with additional analogy problems, a follow-up discussion, or another activity (brainstorming, "What would happen if . . . ?", or others). However, do not allow a session to end too quickly—encourage children to "Put on your thinking caps" and "dig a little deeper" for comparisons.

Getting Started

Remind children of the meaning of "analogical thinking": It's thinking about how things are alike. Use examples: Stars are like little lights. A zebra is like a horse. Ice cream is like snow.

Explain that we are going to think about our rights and others' rights to fair and pleasant treatment by using analogies—by making comparisons. Encourage children to use their creative imaginations to come up with as many comparisons as they can.

Introduce the problem: "How is a _____ like a _____ ?" If someone makes a comparison that is unclear, explain the comparison or ask the child to do so.

Be sure to record ideas on the chalkboard or have a student volunteer write them.

A small-group format, groups of 2 to 6, can be used. Children would be given 2–4 minutes (or more, if needed) to think of at least one analogy. Groups then report to the class. Groups may work on the same or different analogy problems.

Follow-Up

After EACH analogy problem, review the comparisons and emphasize and explain the particular points of similarity.

There are many possibilities for follow-up exercises with analogy problems. As noted in Chapter 10, the adult can ask children to make up their own analogies. On the chalkboard write, "**A helpful person** (or rude person, good friend, person who cheats, steals, is rude, is a bully, is polite, loses his/her temper, never shares, never helps at home, makes messes for others to clean up, etc.) **is like** _____." Children can volunteer answers in an oral exercise. They can spend 5 or 10 minutes writing answers at their desks or tables, then report them. Small groups can work at creating different analogy problems.

A teacher or parent also can improvise novel analogical comparisons on the spot. For example, "**How is somebody who doesn't care about others rights like a** . . . (broken bicycle, a broken piano, a dog who snarls and bites, a drunk driver, a stack of Monopoly money)?"

For a quick follow-up, the two parts of many analogies can be recombined, for example:

How is being treated unfairly like a flat tire on a bicycle? (20.1 + 20.4)

How is a friendly, helpful person like a hot fudge sundae? (20.2 + 20.3)

How is helping others like a fine orchestra? (20.3 + 20.2)

How is pleasantness like a strawberry shortcake? (20.8 + 20.11)

With all analogy problems be sure that our rights and the rights of others—to fair and civilized treatment—are clear. Where appropriate, emphasize the point of view of any victim(s) and try to elicit commitments to positive attitudes and behavior.

Is it good to understand our rights? Why?

Is it good to understand that other people have rights? Why?

Do people who ignore our rights—who are unfair and unpleasant to us—make good friends? Why not?

What do we think of people who ignore our rights?

What would we think of ourselves if we ignored other people's rights? Would we respect ourselves a lot?

Is it good to respect others' rights? Why?

Will people think we are good citizens if we respect others' rights?

Are you someone who will respect others' rights?

Analogical Thinking Problems About Our Rights, Others' Rights

Problem 20.1   Mr. Jones is playing softball with five boys and you—you are a girl. He gives each of the boys several turns at bat, but he ignores you, which definitely is not fair. How is being treated unfairly like sticking your finger in a light socket?

Problem 20.2   Your friend Lashanda loves to help people. She helps you with homework. She helps her parents and neighbors with chores. How is a friendly, helpful person like a fine orchestra?

Problem 20.3   How is helping others like a hot fudge sundae?

Problem 20.4.   How is being rude to people like a flat tire on a bicycle?

Problem 20.5.   Terrell is a very caring boy. He is extra nice to new students and students with disabilities. He visits with his grandmother and senior citizens in the neighborhood and talks to them about their lives. How is a caring person like a rainbow?

Problem 20.6.   When someone calls you names or is rude to you, it hurts your feelings doesn't it. How is being rude like a bad dream or nightmare?

Problem 20.7   People are different in many ways. How are differences between people like the pieces in a picture puzzle?

Problem 20.8   We like it when people are pleasant to us. How is pleasantness like comics in the newspaper?

Problem 20.9. Imagine that your neighbor doesn't like children, and so he yells at you every chance he gets. How is being yelled at (for no reason) like putting your money in a candy machine—and nothing comes out?

Problem 20.10 Your friend Jack always cheats at Monopoly and other games. How is being cheated like a swimming pool with no water in it?

Problem 20.11 How is being fair to friends and family like eating a great strawberry shortcake?

Problem 20.12 How is taking good care of your pet like caring for an expensive bicycle?

Problem 20.13 How is being rude to people like putting a killer piranha into a goldfish bowl?

Problem 20.14 How is being rude like sticking your hand on a hot stove?

Problem 20.15 Imagine you are an elderly person. How is a rude child like a mad dog?

Problem 20.16 Imagine you a student with a disability; perhaps you cannot see very well or have trouble reading. How are rude classmates like a broken arcade game?

Problem 20.17 Again, imagine you are a student with a disability; perhaps you cannot hear very well or cannot do math problems. How are helpful classmates like a new puppy?

Problem 20.18 How is being rude and unpleasant at home like spending the day in an old, old garbage can?

Problem 20.19 How is being rude and inconsiderate in public like an automobile accident?

Chapter

Taking Another Perspective:

"How Does It Feel To Be Cheated?"

_____

Objectives

To give children practice having empathy for others. To help children become "empathy conscious." More specifically, to help children imagine the thoughts and feelings of each person involved in a rights violation episode—particularly the victim, but sometimes the perpetrator and others. To help clarify the impact on victims; the thoughtless lack of empathy of the perpetrator; and the feelings and reactions of others involved (for example, relatives of victims).

Time Required

These guided discussion exercises may elicit just a few answers or may stimulate many relevant ideas and experiences about perceptions and feelings related to having our rights to fair, pleasant treatment violated.

Getting Started

Remind children of the importance of looking at things from other people's viewpoints. Emphasize that "People often treat others badly because they do not look at their hurtful behavior from the victim's point of view. They do not think about the victim's feelings. They do not think about the victim's right to honest and friendly treatment."

Explain that "We're going to practice looking at things from other people's points of view. We will 'get into their shoes.' We will try to understand their thoughts and feelings. Be sure to try hard to 'get inside the heads' of the people in the stories, and imagine their thoughts and feelings."

Read or paraphrase the brief scenario, then ask about the feelings and perceptions of the people in the situation.

Follow-Up

Each exercise includes its own follow-up suggestions. You also may wish to be ready with real-world examples of related misbehavior in which the feelings and rights of the victim were totally ignored. Regrettably, there is no shortage of examples.

Some impromptu "What would happen if . . . ?" questions might encourage additional empathy and perspective-taking. For example, "What would happen if none of us ever thought about anybody else's rights or feelings in this classroom (family, neighborhood)? We insult each other, hurt each other's feelings, and we steal each other's things. How would that be?" "What would happen if nobody EVER considered the rights and feelings of other people? Would the world be pretty awful?"

Taking Other Perspectives

Scenario 21.1. **You Are José, an Ignored Newcomer**

Imagine that you are José, a new boy in class (or in the neighborhood). You are from Puerto Rico. Nobody ever asks you to play softball or any other game. You are never invited to any parties or anything else. You are just ignored.

Well, José, how do you feel? Good? Sad? Lonely?

What do you think about the other children? Are they friendly? Unfriendly? Rude? Considerate?

What are the other children thinking about when they ignore you?

Are they thinking about your feelings?

Are they thinking about your point of view?

Scenario 21.2. **Mr. Thompson Is Treated Badly**

Imagine that you are in middle school in the eighth grade. Mr. Thompson is a new teacher. He teaches math. He is young and not very sure of himself. A few rowdy students deliberately yell at him, argue with him, mess up his desk when he is out of the room, refuse to cooperate, make a lot of noise, and even write insulting notes on the blackboard.

How does Mr. Thompson's feel about this? Is he happy? Sad? Worried?

Are students being fair to Mr. Thompson?

Are the students thinking about Mr. Thompson's feelings?

Do they CARE about Mr. Thompson's feelings? Why not? (No empathy?)

Why are they doing this? Are they thinking only of themselves? Are they "just having fun?"

Does Mr. Thompson deserve respect?

Does Mr. Thompson have a right to pleasant, fair treatment?

Scenario 21.3. **YOU Are the School Teacher**

Imagine that YOU are a school teacher. (Maybe you are Mr. Thompson.)

How do you deserve to be treated by students?

Do you have feelings? Is it fair for students to hurt your feelings?

What rights do you have? (To pleasant and fair treatment; to attention; to cooperation . . .)

Scenario 21.4. **You Are Fran Fremont's Mom**

Imagine that you are Fran Fremont's mother—YOU are Mrs. Fremont. Mr. Fremont doesn't exist; he disappeared years ago. Your daughter, Fran, is rude to you, refuses to help you with any chores, comes and goes as she wishes, stays out late, demands money that you don't have, and gets mad about little things and storms out of the house.

Well, Mrs. Fremont, how do you feel about all of this?

Is Fran thinking about your feelings?

Is Fran taking your point of view on things?

Is Fran treating you fairly?

Do you deserve fair treatment?

Is Fran thinking only of herself and what she wants?

Would YOU ever be like Fran?

Scenario 21.5. **Biff Bulldozer**

Imagine you are Billy, a small child in the second grade. Biff Bulldozer is a big bully—in the fifth grade. He knocks you and other little kids out of the way whenever he wants. Sometimes he takes your lunch and threatens to murder you if you squeal. One day he takes your new gloves and says "You better not tell anybody or you'll get it!"

Well, little Billy, how does it feel to be Biff Bulldozer's victim? Are you happy? Sad? Scared?

What do you REALLY think of Biff?

What do your friends think of Biff?

Your teacher and principal know about Biff. What do you suppose they think of Biff?

Does Biff think about your feelings?

Does Biff care about your feelings?

SHOULD Biff think about your feelings?

Would you ever be like Biff Bulldozer?

Scenario 21.6. **Penny's Big Sister**

Penny's big sister Alice has a bad temper. Alice always yells at Penny, teases her, and won't let her play with the best games and toys.

How do you suppose Penny feels when she is mistreated by her big sister Alice? Is it a good feeling?

Does Alice think about Penny's feelings?

Does Alice look at the situation from Penny's point of view? Why not?

Is Alice being fair to Penny? Why isn't she being fair?

Should you ever be like Alice, the big sister with the bad temper?

Scenario 21.7. **A Friendly Welcome to the Neighborhood**

Imagine that you just moved into a new neighborhood. The people next door come over, introduce themselves, welcome you to the neighborhood, and give you a plate of cookies for your family.

How do you feel? Is it a good feeling?

What do you think of your neighbors?

Do they think about other people's feelings?

Should you be like your neighbors?

Scenario 21.8. **You Are In a Wheelchair**

Imagine that your name is Keneisha. You are in the fifth (fourth, sixth) grade. You were born with a disability, and you cannot walk. You go everywhere in a wheelchair. In your fifth-grade class, everyone is VERY nice to you. Everybody smiles, says hello, and they like to work with you in groups. If you need help, maybe getting something from a high shelf, your friends are quick to say "Hey, wait Keneisha, lemme' help you!"

Do you like the other children in your class? A lot?

How do they make you feel? Happy? Welcome? Good all over?

Do they think about your rights to fair treatment?

Do they think about your rights to pleasant treatment?

Should all children be like the ones in your class?

Visualization About Rights of Others:

"You Are a Hungry Four-Year-Old"

Objectives

These visualization exercises continue the effort to help children empathize—to imagine the feelings, thoughts, and perspectives of others, particularly victims of bad behavior.

Time Required

Introductions and narrations require about 10 minutes. The follow-up discussions of perceptions and feelings may take another 5 or 10 minutes.

Getting Started

Remind children of the importance of understanding other people's feelings, thoughts, and points of view. Remind them that we will be less likely to hurt or mistreat others if we can think about what it is like to be hurt or mistreated.

Have everyone "get comfortable, shut your eyes, and let your imagination come alive. Try to understand the thoughts and feelings of the people in the story(s)." Read or paraphrase the scenarios fairly slowly, with pauses where indicated by ellipses (. . .).

Follow-Up

Each scenario includes its own follow-up questions. After each narration, ask children—in their role as victim or observer of bad behavior—to describe their feelings and perceptions. Be sure to clarify for everyone the thoughts, feelings, and perceptions of the victims of bad behavior, as well as the reactions of others in the story who are affected by the poor values and behavior.

Elicit commitment by asking children to agree that "This behavior (and value) is bad (wrong). It hurts other people. It hurts ourselves."

A problem solving approach might be a helpful follow-up: "What is the problem here?" and "How can we solve it?".

Visualizing About Others' Rights

Scenario 22.1.   **You Are Four Years Old, Your Mother Mistreats You Badly (Based on a true story and is fairly intense.)**

Imagine that YOU are four years old . . . You live in a crowded, dirty apartment with your mother, nine other adults (yes, nine)—and 18 other children (yes, 18) . . . All of the children are under 12 years old . . . Some are babies . . . You are hungry . . . Your mother doesn't seem to care . . . She spends her grocery money on crack cocaine . . . All nine of the adults are addicted to crack cocaine . . . They lie around . . . They act dopey . . . They don't seem to care about any of the children. . . . You wish your mother would love you . . . You wish your mother would take care of you . . . But she just takes drugs . . . Sometimes she yells and swears at you . . . You are very unhappy. . . .

One day the police come. Your mother and the other adults are arrested and put in jail . . . You are scared . . . But the policewomen are very kind to you . . . They hug you and kiss you . . . They give you a bath and some clean clothes . . . You ask one policewoman, "Will you be my mommy?" . . . She can't be your mommy, but later that same day you go to live with foster parents who like you a lot and they take very good care of you . . . You are happy now . . .

When you were hungry and lived in the dirty apartment, how did you feel?

Did the adults have empathy for you? Did they understand your feelings? Why not?

Do you have rights? Do you have the right to be loved? To be cared for?

Did any of the adults care about your rights? Why not?

Should any children EVER be treated this way? Why not?

If you know of children who are treated like this, what should you do?

Scenario 22.2. **You Are the Teacher (a more-or-less humorous approach)**

Imagine that YOU are a new fifth-grade teacher . . . You are at the chalk board trying to explain how to add ½ plus ¼ . . . Nobody is paying any attention AT ALL! . . . Juan is scratching a sore on his ankle . . . Jenny is reading a comic book in her lap . . . Ling-Jen is writing a note to Susan . . . She passes the note . . . Susan reads it and giggles . . . Then Susan wads up the note and throws it at the wastebasket. . . . Kevin is in a back seat folding airplanes . . . He has about 30 so far . . . Leon, Carlos, and Pat are whispering about a new Batman movie . . . Then Nathan walks into class late, and sits down wearing his Walkman earphones . . . You say, "Nathan, please take off the Walkman. Music time isn't until 2:30" . . . But Nathan does nothing—because he can't hear you.

Then you ask Ling-Jen, "How can we add ½ plus ¼? . . . Ling-Jen is startled. She drops the pencil she was writing another note with . . . She answers, "How can we who?" . . . Kevin sails a couple of airplanes across the room . . . Everyone giggles . . . You ask, "Who can solve this problem?" . . . No one knows what you are talking about . . . Everyone looks at you and says, "Huh? What problem?" . . .

Are you, the teacher, being treated fairly or badly?

How do you feel when nobody pays attention? Good? Bad?

Are your students respecting your rights?

Do you have a right to be listened to?

Do students have the right to read comic books, write notes to each others, sail airplanes, talk about movies, walk in late, and wear earphones in class—*while you are trying to teach them?*

What rights do teachers have? (To respect, attention, politeness, good work, . . .)

Scenario 22.3. **Robbing and Beating the Elderly (true story)**

Imagine you are an elderly person . . . You are retired and you live in your small home with your spouse . . . One evening there is a knock on your door . . . You open the door and two young men burst in and one of them pushes you to the floor . . . You look up and see that he has a gun . . . How do you feel? . . . What do you think about? . . . He tells you he wants all of your money . . . All of your credit cards . . . Your wedding rings . . . All of your other jewelry . . . Your cameras . . . Your radios . . . Your small color TV set . . . You explain to him, "I have no money, it's all in the bank" and he hits you very hard with his pistol . . . You find yourself on the floor again . . . You feel blood trickling down your forehead . . .

How do you feel?

Are you frightened? Worried?

What are your thoughts?

Is this sort of robbery and beating all right?

Does it really happen?

Who does this sort of thing?

Do they think about the rights and feelings of the victims?

What do we think of people who do this?

Scenario 22.4. **You Work at McDonald's**

Imagine you have a part-time job at McDonald's . . . It seems like everyone is thoughtless and rude . . . One day you are counting change for a little girl and a loud lady steps in front of the girl and tells you, "I want some ketchup—right now! I'm in a hurry" . . . Then a man demands to know why you don't have any newspapers . . . In a sarcastic voice he says, "Don't you people know how to run a restaurant?" . . . Two teenagers want $20 worth of quarters for the video games next door . . . You explain that you are almost out of quarters, and they look at you and yell "You're a stupid liar!" . . . A young woman wants you to cash a check, but you are not allowed to cash checks . . . She gets mad and yells at you, too . . . Three high school students, two boys and a girl, are drawing pictures on their table—with mustard . . . You hear their cups of ice cubes fall to the floor . . . You know will have to clean up their mess . . .

How do you feel about all of this bad behavior?

Do you feel you deserve respect?

What are your rights as a clerk or counter person?

What kind of people are rude and pushy like the people in this story?

Are they thoughtful? Considerate? Do they have good manners?

Do they think about your feelings? Your point of view?

Do they think about your rights?

What kind of people leave messes for others to clean up?

Are they thoughtful and considerate?

Should you act like these people?

Scenario 22.5. A Bad Day Becomes a Good Day

Imagine that your name is Chris . . . Your day has started badly . . . You are a little sick . . . Maybe it's the pizza, chop suey, and strawberry ice cream you ate last night . . . This morning you couldn't find two socks the same color . . . Oh well, green and purple look nice together . . . Your favorite blue sweater has a couple of new moth holes in it, so you put on an old sweater . . . You wish your sister would get rid of her pet moths . . . At school you slip on the lawn and put a big green grass stain on your tan pants . . . It looks just great! . . . Then you remember that you left your math homework home . . . It was due today, absolutely! . . . Your mother fixed you a SPINACH sandwich for lunch . . . You are NOT in a real happy mood . . .

Then Tawana comes over and says "You look a bit down in the mouth, Chris, cheer up. Come on over after school and we'll listen to some tapes" . . . You smile and say "Okay" . . . You explain to your teacher that you forgot the math assignment . . . The teacher smiles and says, "Gee whiz, I've never forgotten anything in my life! Bring it in tomorrow, air head!" . . . You're beginning to feel a lot better! . . . After you sit down, Jan says "Say, that's a good looking sweater . . . I like it better than your blue one!" . . . Miguel smiles and says, "Hi Chris, have some peanuts! That's a nice looking grass stain" . . . You say, "Thanks, my mom's going to like it, too" . . . Somehow, your troubles don't seem so bad any more. . . .

How do you feel when people are smiling, helpful, and friendly?

Are they respecting your right to friendly treatment?

How do you feel when people are grouchy and unpleasant?

Are they respecting your rights?

Do you like people who are friendly and helpful?

What do you think of people who are grouchy and unpleasant?

Should we try to smile, be friendly, and help others? Is it important?

Are good friends important? Why?

Questions and Discussion About Rights

Objectives

To increase awareness and understanding about our own rights and others' rights. To foster commitment to respecting others' rights.

Time Required

If a rights issue is simple and clear, a few minutes (even seconds) may adequately cover a particular discussion. Ten to 20 minutes might be spent on sets of related questions. More time would be needed if a teacher or parent follows up with a brainstorming or "What would happen if . . . ?" problem.

Getting Started

Little is needed beyond an introduction that orients children to the purpose of the discussion. For example, "We're going to think about our rights and others rights. How we like other people to respect our rights, and why we should respect other people's rights."

Note: Most of the 30 brainstorming problems in Chapter 18 could be used as discussion questions in this chapter. To save space and reduce insults from nit-picking book reviewers, the brainstorming questions in Chapter 18 are not duplicated here.

Discussion Questions About Rights

23.1   We have decided that we all have the right to be treated fairly and nicely, correct? What does "fair treatment" mean?

23.2   What are some examples of fairness?

23.3   What are some examples of being treated unfairly? (Why is that "unfair"?)

23.4   Is fairness important? Why?

23.5   What do we think of people who are unfair?

Do they think of the feelings and rights of others?

Or do they only think of themselves?

23.6.   *Are you someone who likes to be unfair to others?*

Do you cheat in games? Do you grab the biggest piece of cake? Do you grab the best chair or best toys for yourself? Do you always have to be first in getting ice cream cones and getting into the car? Are you greedy and selfish? Do you steal other people's things? Do you damage others' property?

23.7   *Do you respect others' rights?* Are you fair? Do you like to share things? Are you pleasant and friendly? Polite?

23.8   Do animals have rights? What are their rights?

23.9   Do animals have feelings? Do they feel pain? Hunger?

Should we take good care of our pets? Why?

23.10   Imagine that YOU are somebody's pet cat. Would you want to be well taken care of well? How do you feel when your master forgets to feed you or give you fresh water? Is it a good feeling?

23.11   You have rights to fair and friendly treatment. Do people sometimes violate these rights? Are people sometimes unfair or unfriendly? Tell us about it.

23.12   New students have rights. They have the right to be made welcome in our class, and to be treated fairly and in a friendly way. What are some ways to make a new student feel welcome?

23.13   Our parents have rights. Should we make lots of work for our parents—should we ignore dirty dishes? Mess up clean floors? Throw our dirty clothes and towels wherever we want?

How could we show our parents that we respect their right to fair treatment from us?

23.14 Should we waste our parents' money by tearing a new coat that cost $100? By getting grease marks on new school clothes? By dropping an expensive radio?

Do these things show respect for our parents' rights?

23.15 Imagine that YOU are a parent. How do you feel when your child makes messes that you must clean up? Is it a lot of fun? Is your child being thoughtful and considerate? Is your child showing respect for your rights?

23.16 If YOU were a parent, would you enjoy being yelled at or treated rudely by your child? Why not?

Should parents ever be yelled at?

Should they ever be treated rudely?

23.17 Are good friends important? Why?

What rights do our friends have?

Should we be pleasant with friends? Honest and fair?

What happens to our valuable friends if we cheat them, lie to them, steal from them, or treat them rudely?

23.18 Do store clerks have any rights? What are their rights?

If you were a store clerk, would you like to be insulted, yelled at, or complained at?

Would you like to have your store messed up by thoughtless children and teenagers? Why not?

Should we treat clerks and cashiers with respect and friendliness?

23.19 What about the elderly? Do they have a right to dignity and decent treatment?

Word Search and Crossword Puzzles About Rights

The next pages present two word search puzzles and one crossword puzzle about rights. The puzzles are on separate pages so a teacher may copy and use them with the class. A parent may copy them so that children do not write in the book. The solutions are at the end of the chapter.

Word Search About Rights

This word search puzzle is about PEOPLE who have rights.

EVERYONE has rights—rights to be treated fairly, honestly, and in a nice and friendly way. And don't forget, pets are people, too, and they have rights.

People around us, who have rights that we should respect, are hidden in the block of letters. The words are printed left to right or top to bottom. One word is printed upside down, from bottom to top.

Find these words and draw a ring around them.

Parents	Step-Dad	Step-Sis	Custodians
Brothers	Sisters	Store Clerks	Teachers
Bus Driver	Friends	New Kids	Pets	Neighbors

```
S T O R E C L E R K S N
G R D V Q L P K N I I N
B Y X T E A C H E R S E
U L N F W Q Y O C X T W
S X B R O T H E R S E K
D Z F I H J A T V Z R I
R S T E P D A D S N S D
I W J N E I G H B O R S
V Q E D Z T X P F I Y S
E M V S T E P S I S B T
R T K P A R E N T S S E
C U S T O D I A N S H P
```

Another Word Search About Rights

This word search puzzle has words related to our rights and others' rights. The words are about respecting each others' rights to be treated fairly, honestly, and in a friendly way. Some words are related to violating others' rights—being unfair, dishonest, and unfriendly.

The words are printed left to right or top to bottom. One word is printed backwards, from right to left.

Find these words and draw a ring around them.

Rights	Respectful	Fair
Honest	Friendly	Cruel
Rude	Cheating	Name Calling
Teasing	Bully	Helpful

```
T  E  A  S  I  N  G  N
C  R  U  E  L  X  Y  A
H  E  L  P  F  U  L  M
E  S  Z  K  R  R  H  E
A  P  F  W  I  I  O  C
T  E  A  L  E  G  N  A
I  C  I  P  N  H  E  L
N  T  R  M  D  T  S  L
G  F  T  W  L  S  T  I
R  U  D  E  Y  Y  N  N
Y  L  L  U  B  X  F  G
```

Crossword Puzzle About Rights

This is a crossword puzzle about rights.

Crossword puzzles can be fun—and sometimes difficult!!

Write the answers or ideas in the "checkerboard," with one letter in each square. Start each answer in the square that has the same number as the question.

Most of the words are related to our rights and others' rights. But a few are not.

Write "Across" words in the regular way, from left to right.

Write "Down" words from top to bottom (vertically).

ACROSS

1. Violating others' rights is not good, it is _____.
3. We have rights to treatment that is fair, friendly, and _____.
6. We have _____ to treatment that is fair, friendly, and honest.
7. Abbreviation for *island*.
8. Your brother and your _____ have rights, too.
10. Is it a good idea to respect each others' rights?
12. Senior citizens have a right to respectful, helpful treatment. Sometimes we refer to senior citizens as "The _____."
15. _____ whiz!
16. The adult at the front of the class, who has the right to politeness, attention, and good work from YOU.

DOWN

2. "Rover," your pet _____, has the right to be cared for.
3. She has her rights, and he has _____ rights.

From *Teaching Values* published by Westwood Publishing Co. © 1996 Gary A. Davis

4.   We have the right to be treated _____. (Rhymes with *micely* and *twicely*.)

5.   We should not violate other children's rights by poking fun at them or annoying them. That is, we should not _____ them. (Rhymes with *freeze*.)

6.   We want our rights to be respected, and so we should _____ other people's rights.

9.   When people tease us or are rude to us, it doesn't make us happy, it make us _____.

11.   We like it fried, scrambled, poached, or boiled, and it has something to do with a chicken.

13.   "Rah, _____, sis, boom, bah!"

14.   If you have an animal, a fish, or bird at home, it is your _____ and it has a right to be cared for.

Solutions To Puzzles In This Chapter

Word Search About Rights

```
S T O R E C L E R K S
                      I     N
B       T E A C H E R S     E
U       F               T   W
S     B R O T H E R S   E   K
D       I               R   I
R S T E P D A D         S   D
I       N E I G H B O R S   S
V       D                   S
E       S T E P S I S   S   T
R       P A R E N T S       E
C U S T O D I A N S         P
```

Another Word Search About Rights

Solution To Crossword Puzzle About Rights

25

Rights Quiz:

Can You Get the Right Answers?

Let's take a Rights Quiz to see if you understand others' rights and our own rights.

Check "True" or "False."

		True	False
1.	Leroy is bigger than Nan. So Leroy has the right to push Nan around whenever he wants.	☐	☐
2.	Even if Nan is small, she has the right NOT to be bullied.	☐	☐
3.	Fred stole your boom box. Fred respects your rights.	☐	☐
4.	Fred does not have a boom box. So Fred has the right to steal yours.	☐	☐

	True	**False**
5. Juanita is from Puerto Rico. Leroy calls her names. He tells her to "Go back where you came from!" Leroy respects Juanita's rights.	☐	☐
6. Juanita is a nice person, just like you. She has a right to be treated nicely.	☐	☐
7. If Leroy is in a bad mood, he has the right to be rude and cruel to Juanita.	☐	☐
8. You are crabby. When your teacher asks you to do things, you pull faces and say "Oh crap!". You are showing respect for your teacher's right to be treated nicely.	☐	☐
9. Shawana makes messes in the class. The teacher, custodian, or other children have to clean up her messes. Shawana has lots of respect for others people's rights.	☐	☐
10. Sarita lied to you. She said that "Our teacher doesn't like you." This hurt your feelings and made you feel very bad. Sarita has a right to lie to you and make you feel bad if she wants to.	☐	☐

	True	False
11. One day you were not home. Your big sister snooped through all of your drawers and boxes. She has a right to snoop through your things.	☐	☐
12. Latricia was in a car accident. Now she must use a wheelchair. You tell your friends that "She's crippled! She doesn't belong in our class!" You are showing respect for Latricia's right to be treated nicely and fairly.	☐	☐
13. Doak has trouble reading. Jan says, "Doak's a dummy. He belongs in a school for dummies!" Jan is showing respect for Doak.	☐	☐
14. One night, Jack, Crystal, Roberto, and Joel broke some school windows. They also spray painted the sidewalk. They had a right to do this because they don't like the principal.	☐	☐
15. Your mom gets you off to school, then she goes to work. You try to help as much as you can. You believe your mom works hard and has a right to some help.	☐	☐
16. Understanding your own rights and respecting other people's rights is a VERY good idea.	☐	☐

Score: If you understand that YOU have rights and OTHERS have rights, you marked "True" to numbers 2, 6, 15, and 16." You marked "False" to all of the others (1, 3, 4, 5, 7, 8, 9, 10, 11, 12, 13, and 14).

How did you do?

Do you understand other people's rights?

Do you understand your rights?

AND . . . Check any items you missed. Maybe you did not understand the statement.

Part V

Personal Development

26

Personal Development:

The "Potpourri" Section

Potpourri. (French: _pot_, a pot + _pourri_r, to rot; lit. a rotten pot). A medley or miscellany; any mixture, esp. of unrelated objects, subjects, etc.

The Personal Development Category Of Values

In addition to _Personal Development_, the other categories of values in this book are _Honesty, Rights of Others, Manners, School And Work Habits_, and _Energy And Environment_. Some years ago, when your author originally attempted to classify specific values, many fell neatly into those categories. However, some extremely important values did not. They were a Raggedy Andy bunch with little in common, and thus was born the category entitled _Personal Development_—a true "potpourri" assemblage of values. It includes:

Accepting Responsibility	Accepting Consequences
Valuing Health, Hygiene	Respect, Self-Respect, Pride
Compassion	Valuing Friends, Treating Them
Controlling One's Temper	Well
Sense of Fair Play, Democracy	Caring for Animals

Most of the values and categories of values treated in this book overlap in meaning. Particularly, *respecting others' rights* implies the majority of the other values. The specific values in our Personal Development, potpourri category will overlap with values that appear in other sections.

Because of the greater diversity of values in this Personal Development section, the possibilities for activities also are greater than in other sections of this book.

"What Would Happen If ...
Teachers Were Irresponsible?"

Objectives

This and the following chapters in this section try to increase awareness and logical understanding of, and personal commitments to, these beneficial values:

Accepting Responsibility   Accepting Consequences

Valuing Health, Hygiene   Respect, Self-Respect, Pride

Compassion   Valuing Friends, Treating Them

Controlling One's Temper   Well

Sense of Fair Play, Democracy   Caring for Animals

Time Required

Each "What would happen if . . . ?" exercise should require about 3 to 10 minutes, depending upon the problem and children's interest. Introductions and follow-ups add to the time requirement.

Getting Started

Discuss the meaning of the particular value, with emphasis on the effects upon others and ourselves. To set the stage, you might ask for definitions of the value and/or examples or personal experiences related to the value.

Explain that "We are going to think about what happens as a result of wrongful behavior. We are going to think about other people's feelings and things that can happen to others and ourselves as a result of poor behavior and bad decisions."

Explain that "The problem will begin with 'What would happen if . . . ?' and you can use your imagination to think about what happens when people make little mistakes and BIG mistakes in their lives."

Whenever possible, stress **rights of others** and **our own rights** ("Does he or she have a right to do this?"); elicit **empathy** ("How does it feel when . . . "); and elicit **commitments** to constructive values and behavior ("Are you the kind of person who will . . . ").

As mentioned in earlier chapters, ideas may be stimulated by suggesting specific contexts: At home? In your own room? In your neighborhood? In the classroom? In the gym, shop, cooking, or art classes? In shopping centers and stores? On the bus? And so on. Watch for pairs or groups of exercises that might be used together.

Follow-Up

One or more follow-up questions are suggested after each problem.

"What Would Happen If . . . ?" Problems in the "Personal Development" Category

RESPONSIBILITY

(Explain the meaning of "being responsible." It means being dependable and trustworthy; doing what we are expected to do; accepting consequences of our actions; and being accountable for what we do.)

Problem 27.1   **What would happen if nobody behaved responsibly at home?** Your mom or the people taking care you do not care for the house, do laundry, fix meals, clean up messes, nor do anything else they are supposed to. What would your home be like?

Would you be happy?

Should people be responsible and do a good job?

Problem 27.2 **What would school be like if teachers were irresponsible?** If they didn't bother to do their job right? Maybe sometimes they wouldn't bother to show up. Maybe they were never ready for class. Maybe they wouldn't help you in class. What would school be like?

Would it be fair to children if teachers were irresponsible?

Problem 27.3 **What would happen if all children were irresponsible?** You all refuse to help at home. You refuse to pay attention and learn anything in school. You never clean up any messes. You never cooperate with your mom. You never cooperate with the teacher. What would happen?

Is it a good idea to be responsible? To cooperate at home and in school? To take care of messes we make? To try to do a good job? Why?

Problem 27.4 **What would happen if bus drivers were irresponsible?** Maybe they are always late. Maybe they get a little drunk before they pick up the kids. Maybe they don't care about doing a good job, they just want to go home and watch TV. What would happen?

Are we glad our bus drivers are responsible?

Should everyone try to be responsible people?

Problem 27.5 **What would happen if your doctor were irresponsible?** What would happen if your doctor didn't pay any attention to what he or she were doing? Maybe your doctor goes out to play golf instead of showing up for your eye surgery? What would happen?

Are we glad doctors are responsible?

Problem 27.6 **What would happen if nobody would accept responsibility for their bad behavior?** Everybody felt they could be nasty to other people or could damage other people's things without worrying about being answerable for what they did. What would happen?

Is being responsible and trustworthy important?

Should we all be responsible? Do what we are expected to do? Try to do a good job? Accept the consequences for our misbehavior?

HEALTH AND HYGIENE

Problem 27.7 **What would happen if nobody took care of their health?** Nobody gets any exercise. We all eat nothing but candy and potato chips—no milk or fruit or vegetables. We don't get any shots to protect against diseases. We expose ourselves to people with contagious diseases. What would happen?

Why is our health important?

Problem 27.8 **What would happen if nobody ever came to school clean?** No baths, no clean clothes, an inch of dirt and germs all over you. What would happen?

Is cleanliness important?

COMPASSION

Problem 27.9 **What would happen if nobody ever cared about anyone but themselves?** What would happen if everybody said things like, "It's okay if our neighbors have problems and suffer, I'm too busy to help!" or "I have my problems, they have their problems; they can take care of themselves!"? What would happen?

How would you feel if nobody would help you when you needed help?

If we refused to help others, what kind of people would we be?

Are you the kind of person who will help people?

VALUING FRIENDS, TREATING FRIENDS WELL

Problem 27.11 **What would happen if none of us had any friends?** (Maybe we are so obnoxious or rude or dishonest that nobody likes us.) What would happen?

Are friends valuable?

Should we treat friends well (fairly, nicely, honestly)?

SELF-RESPECT, RESPECT FROM OTHERS

Problem 27.12 **What would happen if no one wanted to be proud of themselves?** No one cares about self-respect. We all decide it's just fine to be as rotten as we want to be!

How do we get self-respect? What do we have to do so we can be proud of ourselves? (Be honest, pleasant, treat others well, try our best to reach our goals, . . .)

Problem 27.13 **What would happen if everyone wanted to have self-respect and be respected by others?** What would happen if we all wanted to be thought of as friendly, honest, and fair? We all work hard to reach our goals.

Is self-respect and respect from others important to us? Why?

CONTROLLING ONE'S TEMPER

Problem 27.14 **What would happen if nobody ever controlled their temper?** Everyone just gets mad at everybody else at the slightest little thing?

Would you be happy?

Is it important to control our tempers? To try not to get angry at people?

DEMOCRACY, FAIR PLAY

Problem 27.15 **What would happen if we were always rude and unfair to people who are a little different from ourselves?** Maybe we wouldn't bother to be nice to children who are tall or short, or children whose skin is a different color (because their parents or grandparents came from a different country than our parents or grand-parents)? What would happen if we were always rude and unfair to people who are a little different?

All of us are different from everyone else. We come in all sizes, shapes, and colors and with different skills and abilities. Would we like others to treat us badly because we are a little different in some way?

Is it a good idea to be rude and unfair to children who are a little different? Why not?

Is it better to be kind to people?

What happens when we are kind to people?

Problem 27.16 **What would happen if we always respected and accepted people who happen to be different?** We make it a point to be kind, friendly, and fair to everyone. What would happen?

Would you be a better person if you were kind, friendly, and fair to everyone, even if they are a little different from you?

Does *everyone* have a RIGHT to be treated in a fair and friendly way? Or do some of us have the RIGHT to be rude and cruel to other people?

28

Brainstorming and Reverse Brainstorming with "Personal Development" Topics

---

Objectives

To foster understanding of a miscellany of important values. To help children make commitments to values that help others, themselves, and society.

Time Required

Probably 5 to 15 minutes, depending upon the problem, children's interest, and whether or not it is the last day of school.

Prod children for additional ideas: "Anyone else have an idea?" Ask quieter children, "Darnell, do you have an idea or two?" The adult also can suggest ideas.

Getting Started

If needed, explain the meaning of the particular value, perhaps by asking "What do we mean by 'responsibility' ('good health,' 'self-respect,' 'respect from others,' 'fair play,' 'democracy')?"

Explain that we are going to think about (that topic) by brainstorming all the ideas we can about (that topic).

Review brainstorming rules: "We will think of all the ideas we can; we want a long list of ideas. We won't criticize each other's ideas, because criticism is like punishment."

With Reverse Brainstorming, remind children that "In reverse brainstorming we turn the problem around. We think of how to make a situation WORSE. Reverse Brainstorming helps us understand why some values are bad for others and bad for ourselves."

Be sure to record ideas on the chalkboard, or ask a fast-writing student to record them so they will be available for later discussion.

A teacher may use a large-group or small-group format. With small groups, a group spokesperson reports their ideas (or best ideas) to the class. For variety, brainstorm a problem with the entire class, then break into small groups for an additional problem or two.

Brainstorming and Reverse Brainstorming Problems

Reverse Brainstorming problems are marked with an "(R)."

RESPONSIBILITY

Problem 28.1   How many ways can you show that you are a responsible, dependable, trustworthy person? (At home? At school? In your neighborhood? On a bus? In public? In stores and restaurants?)

Problem 28.2   How many ways can you prove, beyond any doubt, that you are an irresponsible, undependable, and untrustworthy slob? (R) (Sloppy work, forgetting to do things, ducking out at dish-washing time, refusing to cooperate, refusing to help, stealing, vandalizing, lying, . . .)

Problem 28.3   How many ways can you think of to avoid "helping out" with work at home? (R)

What do you think of people who are irresponsible, undependable, and untrustworthy?

Do they make good friends?

Do we want people to be able to trust us? To depend on us?

Should we be responsible and trustworthy?

HEALTH

Problem 28.4   Why is good health important? List all the ideas you can.

Problem 28.5   How many ways can you think of to destroy your health? (R)

Problem 28.6   Why is cleanliness good? List all the ideas you can?

Problem 28.7   How many ways can you think of to become a dirty person? You want to smell bad and be covered with germs. (R)

Is anything more important than our health? Why?

COMPASSION

Problem 28.8   What kinds of problems do elderly people have who live all alone and don't have much money? List all the problems you can think of.

Problem 28.9   How many ways can we think of to help an elderly person who lives alone on a small income?

Problem 28.10   How many kinds of class projects can we think of to help the elderly— maybe senior citizens who live alone or who live together in retirement centers or nursing homes? What would be some good class projects that might help them or cheer them up?

Problem 28.11   Imagine that an 80-year-old man lives next door to you. How many ways can we think of to cause him problems or make him unhappy? (R)

Will you ever become an elderly person?

How would you like to be treated?

What do you think of teenagers who play loud music near where elderly persons live? Is that responsible?

What do you think of teenagers who beat and rob older people who are weak and defenseless? Are these teenagers terrific people?

Do you know what "compassion" means? (It means understanding the feelings of people who have problems, and, if possible, trying to help them. A compassionate person shows sympathy and pity and tries to help people.)

CARING FOR ANIMALS

Problem 28.12 How many ways can you think of that people mistreat or hurt their pets or other animals?

Problem 28.13 How many ways can we think of to make your pet (or someone else's pet) comfortable and happy?

If we were somebody's pet, would we want to be cared for and treated well? Why?

Do pets have a right to good care and treatment?

ACCEPTING RESPONSIBILITY AND CONSEQUENCES

(Be certain that everyone understands the meaning of "consequences." It means *result* or *effect*. It's what happens as a result of our actions. Actions have consequences. Some consequences are VERY bad for us; some are VERY good for us. "Responsibility" is defined in Chapter 27.)

Problem 28.14 Imagine that you tried to steal a pair of socks in a department store (you stuffed them in a coat pocket). How many lies can you think of to try to weasel (get) out of trouble? (R)

Will the people at the store, the police, or your mom believe your lies?

Would it be better to say, "I'm sorry. I made a mistake. I won't do it again," and then just accept the consequences?

Do our actions have consequences?

Should we be careful about our actions?

Problem 28.15 What happens if we pay attention and try to do good work in school? What are some consequences? Think of all the ideas you can.

Problem 28.16 Imagine we all are 16 years old. We are all in high school. What can we do to mess up our lives? (R) (Don't study and learn, drop out, smoke, take drugs, ruin our health, become criminals, join a gang, . . .)

Should we do these things?

Are you going to do these things?

VALUING FRIENDS, TREATING FRIENDS WELL

Problem 28.17 What can we do to lose friends or make people not like us? (R)

Problem 28.18 What can we do to be a good friend?

Problem 28.19 What can we do to cause people to like us and respect us?

> Is it a good idea to treat friends well? (To be helpful, pleasant, honest, trustworthy, . . .)
>
> Is it a good idea to be a good friend?

SELF-RESPECT, RESPECT FROM OTHERS

Problem 28.20 What can we do to earn respect from others? To show that we are "fine" human beings? What can we do so that we will be proud of ourselves and have self-respect.

Problem 28.21 Carl Crumb is a real crummy person. What can Carl Crumb do to make sure that everybody knows he is a no good, crummy, dishonest, irresponsible person? (R)

> Which is best, to have respect from others and respect for ourselves? Or to be like Carl Crumb?
>
> Do you want self-respect? Respect from others?

FAIR PLAY, DEMOCRACY

Problem 28.22 How many ways can you think of to treat everyone fairly and equally?

Problem 28.23 How many ways can you think of to be unfair and mean (cruel) to others (other children, parents, brothers/sisters, store owners, elderly people)? (R)

> Is it a good idea to be fair, to be pleasant with everyone, and to treat everyone equally?

Analogical Thinking:

"How Is Responsibility Like a Good Wrist Watch?"

Objectives

To use analogies to help children think about and make decisions and commitments regarding various "Personal Development" values.

Time Required

Often just a minute or two, perhaps a few seconds. Be ready with additional analogy problems, a follow-up discussion, or other activity. But do not allow a session to end too quickly—encourage children to "Put on your thinking caps" and "dig a little deeper" for comparisons.

Getting Started

Remind children of the meaning of "analogical thinking": It's thinking about how things are alike. Use examples. Ask children for examples.

Explain that we are going use analogies to help us think about (whatever the value topic is). Encourage children to "Think of as many comparisons as you can."

Introduce the problem: "How is a _____ like a _____ ?" If someone makes a comparison that is unclear, explain the comparison or ask the child to do so.

Be sure to record ideas on the chalkboard.

A small-group format can be used. Children would be given two or three minutes (or more) to think of at least one analogy, which is then reported to the class. The group may need to explain the analogy: "A _____ is like a _____ because . . . ." Groups may work on the same analogical problem or different ones.

Analogical Thinking Problems

RESPONSIBILITY, ACCEPTING CONSEQUENCES

(Explain or review the meaning of "being responsible." It means being dependable and trustworthy; doing what we are expected to do; being accountable for what we do; and accepting consequences of our actions.)

Problem 29.1	How is being responsible and dependable—doing what you are asked to do, doing what you are expected to do—like a good wrist watch?
Problem 29.2	When you don't help out at home, how is this like a bike with two flat tires?
Problem 29.3	Some people don't accept responsibility for their actions. If they make a mistake or are caught cheating or stealing, they try to lie their way out of it. They say things like "It wasn't my fault" or "I didn't do it." How is "not accepting responsibility for our actions" like a bunch of hungry mosquitoes.

Is it good to be responsible and dependable?

Is it a good idea to accept responsibility for our actions?

HEALTH

Problem 29.4	How is good health like money in the bank?
Problem 29.5	How is a poor diet like an old wet cardboard box?

COMPASSION

Problem 29.6	How is understanding others' feelings and problems like reading a mystery story? (You try to figure out what is happening, what the story characters are thinking and feeling.)
Problem 29.7	How is helping others like a good video game?

VALUING FRIENDS

Problem 29.10 How are good friends like a pet dog?

Problem 29.11 How are bad friends like Monopoly money?

Problem 29.12 How is being a dependable friend like an "Indiana Jones" or "Batman" movie?

RESPECT, SELF-RESPECT

Problem 29.13 How is self-respect like a terrific ice cream sundae?

Problem 29.14 How is respect from others like a paycheck from a job?

CONTROLLING ONE'S TEMPER

Problem 29.15 How is a bad temper like a volcano?

Problem 29.16 How is a calm, patient person like a rainbow?

Do we like people with bad tempers?

Should you have a bad temper?

CARING FOR PETS

Problem 29.17 How is a pet puppy like a little child?

Does a pet puppy deserve to be cared for?

Does a pet puppy have rights?

Should you take good care of your pets?

30

Taking Another Perspective:

"Imagine That Joanne Has a Learning Disability"

Objectives

To give children practice having empathy. To increase awareness and commitment to several personal development values.

Time Required

Guided discussion exercises may elicit just a few answers or many relevant ideas and experiences about perceptions and feelings.

Getting Started

Remind children of the importance of trying to see things from others' points of view, trying to understand others feelings. "*Having empathy* means putting yourself in someone else's shoes, and trying to understand their thoughts and feelings. We're going to practice having empathy. In the little stories I read, try hard to 'get into the other person's shoes' and imagine their thoughts and feelings."

Read or paraphrase the brief scenario, then ask about the feelings, thoughts, and perceptions of the people in the situation.

Follow-Up

Each exercise includes its own follow-up suggestions. Some impromptu "What would happen if . . . ?" questions might encourage additional empathy and perspective-taking. For example, "What would happen if everyone were irresponsible? If nobody were dependable? If nobody accepted responsibility for making mistakes?"

Taking Other Perspectives

RESPONSIBILITY, DEPENDABILITY

Scenario 30.1. **Janet Jones, Irresponsible Person**

Janet Jones is completely irresponsible and undependable. She's always late. She never returns things. She promises to help and then disappears. She loses things—and she is full of excuses for her behavior: "I wasn't late, your watch is wrong." "I already returned your softball, don't you remember?" "I couldn't help you pick flowers for your grandmother because I didn't feel well." "I didn't lose your book, somebody else must have taken it."

What do Janet's friends probably think of her? Do they trust her? Do they believe her excuses?

What does Janet's mother probably think of Janet's behavior? Do the excuses get a little tiresome?

Should Janet be more responsible? More dependable? More trustworthy?

Should we do what is expected of us?

Should we admit mistakes?

Should we all try to be dependable, trustworthy people?

Or should we all be like Janet?

Scenario 30.2 **Dependable Terrell**

Terrell takes pride in being responsible, dependable, and trustworthy. If he says he will help the neighbor cut the lawn, he shows up and helps cut the lawn. If he borrows something, he returns it promptly and in good condition. He helps out at home whenever his mom asks him to, and without a hassle. If you ask him, he'll just say, "It's just the right way to do things. I like people who are responsible and dependable—you can trust them and count on them to help. It's a good way to be."

Does Terrell seem to have good values?

Would it be nice if everyone were like Terrell?

Should YOU be like Terrell?

CONTROLLING ONE'S TEMPER

Scenario 30.3　**Jeremy Johnson's Bad Temper**

Jeremy Johnson has a bad temper—he gets mad at people much too quickly. And he can get angry and nasty about ANYTHING AT ALL. If his mother asks, "Did you get a chance to clean you room?", Jeremy might snap, "Oh, get off my case! You're always nagging, nagging, nagging! I'll clean my room when I feel like it! Now lay off!" If his friends ask, "Do you want to go for an ice cream cone?", he might say, "Oh crap, ice cream, ice cream, ice cream! You guys always have to have ice cream cones! Gimme a break! That's dumb! Don't you have any better ideas than that?" If a stranger asks, "Would you happen to know what time it is?", Jeremy might snap back, "Oh who cares what time it is! Why don't you get a watch or ask somebody else. It's not my job to tell you what time it is!"

What do Jeremy's friends and family probably think of his temper?

Should Jeremy make an effort to be more pleasant?

How do YOU feel when people get mad at you over nothing?

If you were Jeremy, what would you do about your temper?

COMPASSION, FAIR PLAY

Scenario 30.4.　**Joanne Has a Learning Disability—and Good Friends!**

Imagine that Joanne has a learning disability. She has trouble reading and writing words. Joanne's teacher and her friends are very helpful and understanding and patient. They try to help her with her reading and writing skills. And they help her learn in other ways. They read her school books to her. If she has a test to take, they read the test to her. Instead of writing, she is allowed to give answers to tests by speaking.

If you were Joanne, how would you feel about your teacher and your friends?

Are they understanding? Are they fair-minded?

Is it good to understand other people's problems and be helpful?

Scenario 30.5. You Are Always Left Out

Imagine that you always get left out of things. You are left out of games. When other kids have candy or treats, they seem to forget to share with you.

How do you feel?

Do you like to be left out?

Are you happy when others forget to share with you?

Or are you sad? Are your feelings hurt?

Are the other children treating you fairly?

Should we treat everyone the same?

Should we share with everyone?

Should we be sure not to leave anyone out?

RESPECT, SELF-RESPECT

Scenario 30.6. You Are a Rotten Person

Imagine that you are a rotten person. Rotten to the core. You lie, cheat, and steal. You are short-tempered and rude to most everyone, at least when you can get away with it. You bully the smaller kids. You criticize children with disabilities. You even kick dogs! You don't care about anyone but yourself.

Will your family and your friends respect you?

Will anyone respect you?

Is respect from others important?

Can you respect yourself when you are such a rotten person?

Is it a good idea to be such a rotten person?

Chapter

31

Visualization:
"You Are a Goldfish"

Objectives

To give children practice having empathy—imagining the feelings, thoughts, and perspectives of victims, their friends, family, and others. To raise awareness and strengthen commitment to several values in the "personal development" category.

Time Required

Introductions and narrations require about 10 minutes. The follow-up discussion of perceptions and feelings may require another 10 minutes.

Getting Started

Remind children of the importance of understanding other people's feelings, thoughts, and points of view. Remind them that we will be less likely to hurt or mistreat others if we can think about what it is like to be hurt or mistreated.

Have everyone "Get comfortable, shut your eyes, and let your imagination come alive. Be sure to try to understand the thoughts and feelings of the people in the story." Read or paraphrase the scenarios fairly slowly, with pauses where indicated by ellipses (. . .).

Follow-Up

Each scenario includes its own follow-up questions. After each narration, ask children—in their role as victim or observer of bad behavior—to describe their feelings and perceptions. Be sure to clarify the feelings and perceptions so that all children understand the feelings of the persons who are mistreated, and the feelings of those who observe the mistreatment.

Try to elicit commitment by asking children to agree that "This behavior (and value) is wrong because it hurts other people. It hurts ourselves."

Our problem solving approach might be useful: (1) "What is the problem?" and (2) "How can we solve it?"

Visualization Activities: Personal Development

SELFISHNESS, BULLYING, RUDENESS, BEING INCONSIDERATE,
STEALING, SELF-RESPECT, PRIDE, FAIR PLAY

Scenario 31.1.   Beverly Bulldozer

Biff Bulldozer has a sister, Beverly Bulldozer. . . . Beverly has learned all of Biff's bad values and bad habits. . . . Just like Biff, Beverly is selfish, rude, dishonest, and a bully . . . She only think about herself and what she wants . . . She never think about other people's feelings . . . Most people don't like Beverly very much . . . Except Biff . . . Biff thinks she is a terrific sister . . . After all, she is just like him! . . .

Last night there was just one piece of apple pie in the refrigerator . . . Beverly knew that her mom was saving it for grandmother, but she ate it anyway when nobody was looking . . . This morning Beverly's little sister, Angela, wanted to borrow Beverly's sweatshirt . . . She snapped "No, leave it alone! It's mine!" . . . It's October and the elderly couple next door have a foot of leaves on their small lawn . . . But Beverly won't rake the leaves for them, "That's their problem!" she tells herself . . .

Now Beverly is at school. She is walking down the school hallway . . . A little boy gets in her way, so Beverly shoves him aside . . . She didn't look back when she heard him fall . . .

Beverly likes to scare little kids by threatening to "beat 'em up" . . . Sometimes she'll make smaller children give her their lunch money—"or else!" . . . Beverly likes to steal things, too . . . One day she took a nice pair of gloves from a table in the principal's office . . . Another time she found a purse in the hallway . . . She took the two dollars and the sun glasses that were in it . . . She threw the purse in a trash can . . .

Beverly's problem is that she just don't think about being an honest, helpful, and friendly person . . . the kind of person whom most of us like . . .

Do people respect children like Beverly?

How do we earn respect?

Is it all right to be selfish? Rude? Inconsiderate? A thief?

Is this good behavior?

Would you be proud of yourself if you were like Beverly?

Would you have a lot of respect for yourself if you were like Beverly?

Is it important to have self-respect?

What do you think of bullies who push around smaller children, and maybe steal from them?

Is it fair to mistreat smaller children?

Do bullies like Beverly think about the feelings and rights of smaller children?

Do smaller children have a right to nice treatment from bigger kids?

Should we be like Beverly Bulldozer?

RESPONSIBILITY, ACCEPTING CONSEQUENCES

Scenario 31.2. **Lakyta Jones, the Girl Who NEVER Makes Mistakes**

We all make mistakes, and Lakyta Jones makes mistakes, too . . . But Lakyta Jones NEVER, NEVER admits that she EVER makes a mistake . . . One day her mother sent her to the store for some hot dogs . . . She forgot and bought hamburger instead . . . When she got home, she said to her mother, "YOU made the mistake . . . YOU told me to get hamburger . . . If you wanted hot dogs, you should have said 'hot dogs' . . . I did exactly what you said; I didn't make a mistake" . . . At school, her teacher, Ms. Chen, asked "Who was the first President of the United States . . . Lakyta raised her hand and said, "Abraham Lincoln" . . . Ms. Chen said, "Sorry, Lakyta, you're wrong. The first President was George Washington" . . . But Lakyta quickly added, "Abraham Lincoln WAS the first President of the United States, because my uncle said so. If my uncle is wrong, it's not my fault, it's HIS fault. I didn't make a mistake!" . . . On the way home that day, she bumped into a wire fence and ripped her jeans a little . . . Naturally, she told her mother, "It wasn't my fault. That sharp fence shouldn't have been there. I didn't make a mistake."

Should we admit that we sometimes make mistakes?

Do responsible people admit that they make mistakes?

Is the girl in this story, Lakyta Jones, acting in a responsible way?

Should we be like Lakyta Jones? Or should we accept responsibility when we make a mistake?

HEALTH AND HYGIENE, OBSERVING SAFETY RULES (HUMOROUS, MORE OR LESS)

Scenario 31.3.   You Never Think About Health and Cleanliness

Imagine you are someone who never thinks about health, cleanliness, or safety . . . This morning when you looked in the bathroom mirror you noticed that your teeth were a little green . . . Neat! . . . Anybody can have white teeth, they just have to brush them . . . In the medicine cabinet your mother has some new blue pills . . . You say to yourself, "I'll bet they have a sugar coating," and you pop four of them into your mouth . . . They taste pretty good, for arthritis pills . . . You almost combed your hair today, but it was too tangled . . . You'll probably have to cut it off in another couple of months . . . For breakfast, you were running a little late and so you just had a candy bar, a glass of cola, and a couple of marshmallows . . . "If it tastes good, eat it," you think to yourself . . . Before leaving for school, you discover that the battery in your Walkman earphones is dead . . . So you take the battery out of the smoke alarm in the hallway and put it in your Walkman . . . It sounds good now . . .

On the way to school you come to a busy street . . . You say to yourself, "I bet those cars won't hit me" . . . And you walk into the street pretending not to see the cars . . . The drivers hit their brakes and screech their tires . . . But you were right, they missed you! . . . An elderly man in a pick-up truck fainted with fright when he saw you in the road . . .

At school you run down the hall as fast as you can and slide on the waxed floor . . . You really sail—right into Ms. Taylor, the fifth-grade teacher . . . her books and papers get scattered all over the floor . . . She says, "Please don't run in the hallways" . . . Ms. Taylor is very patient . . . Later, you slide down the hall again to see if you can beat your old record

. . . At recess you tight-rope walk along the top of the monkey bars . . . "I haven't fallen yet," you tell yourself . . .

You notice that your shirt is getting little stiff from dirt and dried sweat . . . But you decide you can get another week out of it before it has to be washed . . . Washing clothes just wears them out . . . In class you begin to itch a little because you haven't taken a bath for three weeks . . . Other children look at each other, point to you, and hold their noses . . . You tell yourself, "It must be a new game or a secret code" . . . You notice that, again today, no one is sitting near you . . .

> Is good health and a good diet important? Why?
>
> Is cleanliness important?
>
> Is it smart to do take chances and do dangerous things? Why not?
>
> What can happen if you take the battery out of the smoke alarm?
>
> What do we think about people like the one in this story?
>
> *Would you like to be the person in this story? Why not?*

CARING FOR ANIMALS, COMPASSION, RESPONSIBILITY

Scenario 31.4. **You Are Gordon the Goldfish**

Imagine that you are a goldfish . . . Your name is Gordon . . . It's about seven o'clock in the evening and you and your goldfish friends are paddling around your goldfish bowl on the classroom book case . . . The teacher and the children have gone home . . . And your water is getting cloudy, heavy, and smelly . . . "We sure could use a change of water," you think to yourself, as you suck in a big gulp . . . "It's hard to get any oxygen out of this muck! . . . They must have forgotten us again!" . . .

Then your friend Ernestine swims over . . . Ernestine looks pretty bad . . . She's tilting a little to one side . . . Her fins twitch a bit . . . She looks a little thin, too . . . "What's up, Ernestine?" you ask, "You look a little pale?" . . . "It's this water!" says Ernestine, . . . "If we don't get a change soon, it'll be 'belly up' time!" . . . "I know exactly how you feel, kid," you reply. "But hang in there, maybe tomorrow they'll remember" . . . Then you add, "A couple of goldfish pellets would taste good, too . . . They forgot to feed us again today" . . . "I know," said Ernestine, "but I guess these guys are just too busy with all their reading, writing, and arithmetic stuff . . . Whew! I'm getting real dizzy! . . . I hope Harriet Hamster and Gwendolyn Guinea Pig are doing better than we are!" . . .

Would you like to be Gordon or Ernestine Goldfish?

How do they feel? Are they happy? Are they being treated fairly?

What rights to pets have?

Do responsible people take care of their pets?

Would you mistreat your pets?

32

Questions and Discussion in the "Personal Development" Category of Values

Objectives

To increase awareness and understanding and elicit commitments regarding responsibility, valuing friends, good health, respect and self-respect, and other "personal development" topics.

Time Required

If an issue is simple, a few minutes (or seconds) may adequately cover a discussion. Ten minutes or more might be spent on interrelated questions. More time would be needed if a teacher or parent follows up with an impromptu brainstorming or "What would happen if . . . ?" problem.

Getting Started

Orient children to the purpose of the discussion. For example, if the topic is responsibility: "We're going to think about how important it is to be responsible and trustworthy. We like people to be responsible and trustworthy with us, and so we should be responsible and trustworthy with others."

Discussion Questions

RESPONSIBILITY

32.1   What is "responsibility"? (Being honest and trustworthy? Being dependable? Accepting consequences? Being accountable for our mistakes and misbehavior?)

32.2   If we are given and job and don't do it, is that being responsible?

32.3   If we promise to do something and then don't do it, is that being responsible?

32.4   If we promise to meet someone and we don't bother to show up, is that being responsible?

32.5   If someone deliberately scratches a table, gouges the restroom wall, drops bubble gum in the fish bowl when nobody is looking, or tears pages out of your book when you are not around, is that person being responsible for his or her behavior?

32.6   Is it fair for people to be irresponsible? To damage things, to be undependable, or to mistreat other people?

32.7   Should we think about consequences of wrong behavior before we do something we know is wrong? Should we think about how we might hurt others? Is it all right to hurt others? Do we like to be hurt?

32.8   What do we think of people who do not take responsibility for their behavior? Are they thoughtful and intelligent? Are they dependable friends?

32.9   Will we like ourselves better if we are responsible people?

HEALTH

32.10   Which is most important, lots of money or good health? Why?

32.11   How many ways can you think of to make your body healthy?

32.12   Is it important to be clean? To take baths regularly and wear clean clothes? Why?

32.13   If we see dirty children in school or on the street, what are our feelings? What do we think? (We might feel sorry for them; we might believe they have bad habits, poor health, or parents who do not care about them.)

COMPASSION

32.14   What is compassion? (Caring about the problems and difficulties of others? Sympathy? Pity? Wanting to help?)

2.15   Is it good to be have compassion? Why?

CONTROLLING ONE'S TEMPER

32.16   What is a "bad temper"? (Getting mad at people over little things? Snapping at people when you shouldn't?)

32.17   Is it ever good to have a bad temper?

32.18   What do we think of people with bad tempers? Do we like them for friends?

FAIR PLAY, DEMOCRACY, RESPECTING DIFFERENCES

32.19   In what ways are people alike?

32.20   In what ways are people different?

32.21   Is it all right to be different? Or does everyone have to be exactly the same?

32.22   What would the world be like if everyone were exactly the same?

32.23.   Does someone who is different deserve respect and dignity? Can we accept them and treat them well? Or is it all right to be rude to them, tease them, hurt their feelings, and leave them out of everything?

32.24   How would (does) it feel to be treated rudely, teased, and left out of activities because you are a little different? Is it a nice feeling?

32.25   Imagine you went to a school where everyone had one arm—but you had two! Everybody is rude to you. They ignore you. They call you "the weirdo with two arms." They don't talk to you. And they leave you out of games and parties because you are so strange—you have two arms instead of one, like everybody else.

How would you feel? Is it a good feeling?

Do you deserve to be treated badly because you have too many arms? Is it fair to you?

32.26   Is it all right to be different?

RESPECT AND SELF-RESPECT

32.27 What is respect? (Thinking highly of someone; being considerate to them; showing courtesy, esteem, high regard.)

32.28 Is it important for others to respect us? Why?

32.29 How do we earn respect at school? At home? In the community?

32.32 What is self-respect? Thinking highly of ourselves? Liking who we are?

32.31 Is it important to have self-respect? To like ourselves? Why?

32.32 Can we like ourselves and respect ourselves if we lie, cheat, steal, or destroy property? Or if we are rude, unpleasant, or cruel to other children? Why not?

32.33 How many ways can you think of to lose your self-respect?

32.34 Is respect from others related to self-respect? How?

32.35 What is pride? Is it important? Is it like self-respect?

32.36 Can we be proud of ourselves if we lie, cheat, steal, or vandalize others' property? Or if we are bullies? Or unfair to others? Or if we are bad-tempered, rude, and nasty to other children or our parents?

32.37 Is it good to earn respect from others?

32.38 Is it good to have self-respect?

33

Word Search and Crossword Puzzles:

Personal Development

The next pages present
two word search puzzles
and one crossword puzzle
dealing with values in the
"personal development"
category. The puzzles are
on separate pages so a
teacher or parent may
copy them.

The solutions are at the
end of this chapter.

Values Word Search

This word search puzzle is about lots of important values.

Words related to responsibility, treating friends well, good health, respect, fair play, and some others are hidden in the block of letters. The words are printed left to right or top to bottom. One word (or phrase) is printed from right to left.

Find these words and draw a ring around them.

Compassion	Fair Play	Good Diet
Responsible	Respect	Do Jobs Well
Differences	Trustworthy	

```
R E S P E C T D
E Z F D S O R O
S B A I K M U J
P X I F T P S O
O C R F R A T B
N V P E N S W S
S J L R X S O W
I W A E Q I R E
B Y Y N M O T L
L L R C H N H L
E Q D E W K Y Z
M T J S U H Q R
T E I D D O O G
```

Another Search For Values Words

This is another word search puzzle about responsibility, friends, health, respect, fairness, and some others. The words are printed left to right or top to bottom.

Find these words and draw a ring around them.

Friends	Pride
Health	Self-Respect
Temper	Fairness
Cleanliness	Exercise

```
C X F R I E N D S
L U A D P R I D E
E L I S Z B N O L
A Y R Z I Q R C F
N P N T E M P E R
L M E X F Q Y K E
I V S N G W U J S
N B S T P K H N P
E X E R C I S E E
S M A Z W Q C V C
S H E A L T H I T
```

Crossword Puzzle: Values Words

This is a crossword puzzle. Most of the words are related to responsibility, friends, health, respect, self-respect, and fairness. But a few words don't have anything to do with anything.

Write the answers or ideas in the "checkerboard," with one letter in each square. Start each answer in the square that has the same number as the question.

Write "Across" words in the regular way, from left to right.

Write "Down" words from top to bottom (vertically).

ACROSS

1. Someone who tries to be fair has a good sense of "_____ _____." (Two words; rhymes with *bear day*.)

4. A _____ person is dependable, trustworthy, shows up on time, does jobs well, and accepts consequences for his or her actions.

6. Edward's nickname.

8. People who eat nutritious food, get exercise, and don't smoke are taking care of their _____.

9. Joe gets mad at everybody quickly. Joe has a bad _____.

10. Abbreviation for Los Angeles.

12. Louise has lots of sympathy, understanding, and pity for people. Louise has _____. (Rhymes with *dumb-fashion*.)

16. A "good diet" means that you _____ well.

18. A "good diet" means that you eat _____.

19. _____-respect.

DOWN

1. _____ are very valuable. We should treat them well. (Rhymes with *blends*.)

2. When you "think ahead" that means you _____ things. (Rhymes with *fan*.)

3. If you take baths and wear clean clothes, that means you believe _____ is a good value. (Rhymes with *friendliness*.)

5. If we have good values, we can take _____ in ourselves. (Rhymes with *bride*.)

7. Opposite of "bottom."

8. Opposite of "him."

11. A responsible person tries to do a good _____.

13. Initials of Abraham Lincoln.

14. Initials of one of Columbus' ships.

15. Initials of our favorite *Extra-Terrestrial*.

17. A very important person; and the post office abbreviation for Maine.

From *Teaching Values* published by Westwood Publishing Co. © 1996 Gary A. Davis

Solutions to Puzzles in This Chapter

Values Word Search

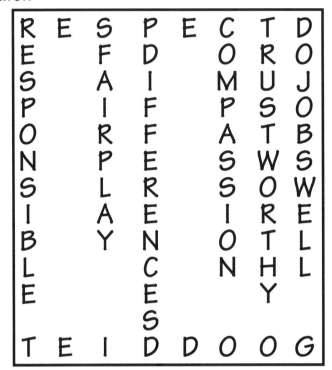

Another Search For Values Words

Crossword Puzzle

Arithmetic Test:

"Let's Subtract Tyler!"

Imagine that Tyler is a dishonest, unfair person. You might call him a *crook*. Tyler steals everything. He lies to everybody. He cheats in every game. He breaks promises. He vandalizes and breaks other people's things. And he NEVER returns anything!

Here are some arithmetic problems about Tyler.

The answers are at the end of this chapter.

1.   You have 4 friends, Jackie, Chris, Bobbie—and Tyler!

 a.   How many *good* friends to you have? _____

 b.   How many friends can you trust? _____

Jackie, Chris, Bobbie, Tyler

_____ - Tyler _____

?

2.　　You received 8 new cassettes for your birthday. Tyler comes over for a visit. Now you have 6 new cassettes. How many cassettes do you believe are in Tyler's pocket? _____

3.　　Your teacher, Mr. Gonzales, gives a spelling test. There are 10 words. Then he asks five people (you, Jackie, Chris, Bobbie, and Tyler), "How many words did you spell correctly?" (It was a hard test.)

You say "7."

Jackie says "8."

Chris says "6."

Bobbie says "7."

Tyler says "10—I got 'em ALL right!"

You, Mr. Gonzales, and everybody else knows that Tyler can't spell his own name!

a.　　How many people will think Tyler is a dishonest liar? (Don't forget yourself and Mr. Gonzales.) _____

b.　　How many people will lose respect for Tyler? _____

> Here's how Tyler usually spells:
>
> "Misster rabit ayt hiz carotz."

4.　　On Monday Jackie loans five valuable books. Jackie loans one to you, one to Chris—and three to Tyler. Jackie asks all of you to return them on Thursday. On Friday, how many books does Jackie have? _____

5.　　You are getting smarter about friends. Of Jackie, Chris, Bobbie, and Tyler, how many are no longer your friends? _____

6. Imagine that you, Jackie, Chris, Bobbie, and Tyler are in high school. Tyler drops out and watches TV all day. The rest of you graduate and go on to college or a technical school.

   a. When you are all 30 years old, how many will have a good job and earn good pay? (Don't forget to count yourself.) _____

   b. How many will WISH they had stayed in school? _____

7. In high school, Tyler has some new friends. Two of them are burglars and steal things. Two others sell drugs. Two more break windows, set fires, and chop down little trees at the school.

   a. How many will probably be arrested by the police?

      (Don't include Tyler, yet.) _____

   b. How many will be embarrassed and feel awful when the police talk to their parents? _____

   c. How many might be sent to a juvenile detention center? _____

      Do you respect Tyler?

      Yes _____ No _____

      Would you like to be like Tyler?

      Yes _____ No _____

      Would the world be a mess if EVERYONE were like Tyler?

      Yes _____ No _____

Answers to arithmetic problems:

1a.	3	3a.	5	5 .	1	7a.	6
b.	3	b.	5	6a.	4	b.	6
2 .	2	4 .	2	b.	1	c.	6

Part VI

Manners

Critical Early Manners:

Sharing and Taking Turns

This section is not a Complete Guide to Children's Manners. It covers just a sample of items that seem basic to social behavior. "Manners" in this Section will mean:

Asking (e.g., to borrow things)

Waiting, Patience

Being Courteous, Pleasant, Respectful

Sharing

Behaving "Properly" in Public (Respecting Others' Rights)

Being Considerate With The Elderly and Persons With Disabilities

Doing Favors, Helpfulness

For Parents: Early Social Rules of Taking Turns and Sharing

Before we turn to "What would happen if . . . ?", Brainstorming, and other activities, let's look at two important pre-kindergarten values. Psychologists who specialize in early childhood development emphasize that **sharing** and **taking turns** are two forms of manners (or values) that pre-kindergarten children WILL carry with them into elementary school and beyond. Both *sharing* and *taking turns* are early forms of respecting others' rights and being considerate, fair, and democratic-minded. Critical values indeed!

Little Roberta is five years old. In her kindergarten class she will not allow others to be first, for example, in getting their paints. SHE wants to be first—and she will push and grab and get upset if she does not get her way. She will not share building blocks, crayons, dinosaur models, or other materials. If she likes something, she wants it for herself. Roberta does not understand "taking turns" nor "sharing."

Taking Turns

Taking turns is sufficiently simple that parents can begin to teach this value during their child's very first year. Reminders such as "Now let's take turns" should continue during the following pre-kindergarten years as well.

The game of *peek-a-boo*—which most parents play with their baby anyway—introduces the infant to the principle of taking turns. Initially, mother (or father) plays the game by covering the baby with a light blanket. When the blanket is removed, the parent expresses great surprise with a big "PEEK-A-BOO!" Then the parent can cover his/her own face, remove the blanket, and again "PEEK-A-BOO!" And then it's baby's turn again. An elementary form of taking turns is learned

In one variation, as baby learns this game the baby covers his or her own face, and the parent expresses a big "PEEK-A-BOO!" when baby's face reappears. Parent and baby take turns covering the baby. Another variation is hiding baby's face behind a ball or other toy, with "PEEK-A-BOO!" again following the reappearance of baby's face. Then the parent hides his/her own face behind the ball, and pops out with another "PEEK-A-BOO!" They take turns. Or mom (or dad) can hide behind a doorway, then stick her (his) head out and "PEEK-A-BOO!" Then baby can hide (e.g., behind a pillow), stick its head out, and mom (dad) again exclaims "PEEK-A-BOO!"

You probably can think of other games and activities that can use taking turns. For example, when baby is old enough to hold a spoon, mom and baby can take turns feeding baby a spoonful of delicious strained spinach. Also, you can roll a ball back and forth, with a verbal "Your turn!", "My turn!", and so on.

The principle of taking turns should continue as the child grows through its early years:

"Let's take turns. It's your turn to pull the string (on the talking toy) . . . Now it's my turn . . . Thank you!"

"It's daddy's turn to hug Teddy Bear . . . Now it's your turn . . . Thank you. Isn't it fun to take turns?"

Research shows that children who learn the concept of taking turns at an early age are more likely to take turns when they later play with other children.

Sharing

Sharing is another simple and central social skill that parents can help their child master very early. Like taking turns, the idea of sharing can begin during the first year and continue throughout early childhood.

It's probably obvious, but the way to teach your child the idea of sharing is just to give the child lots of examples of sharing:

"Let's share the blocks. Here's some for you and here's some for me!"

"Here's some apple for you. Here's some for Teddy Bear. And here's some for me. Isn't it fun to share the apple?"

"Let's share the balls. Here's a ball for you. Here's a ball for big sister. And here's a ball for daddy."

"Here's a car for me and here's a big truck for you."

The words *share* and *take turns* are fairly abstract. With toddlers, their meanings can be taught only by concrete experience in sharing and taking turns. Be sure to say "let's share" and "let's take turns" whenever possible. Your child will need to know these meanings and have these values the minute he or she walks into a nursery school or kindergarten.

"What Would Happen If ...

Everybody Just Grabbed?"

_____

Objectives

As noted in Chapter 35, the activities in each chapter of this section focus on increasing children's logical understanding of, and personal commitments to, values related to these kinds of manners:

> Asking (e.g., to borrow things)
>
> Waiting, Patience
>
> Being Courteous, Pleasant, Respectful
>
> Sharing
>
> Behaving "Properly" in Public (Respecting Others' Rights)
>
> Being Considerate With The Elderly and Persons With Disabilities
>
> Doing Favors, Helpfulness

Many of these overlap with values discussed in earlier sections.

Time Required

Three to 10 minutes per activity, depending upon the problem and children's interest. Introductions and follow-ups add to the time requirement.

Getting Started

Discuss the meaning of the particular manners concept, with emphasis on the effects upon others and ourselves. You might ask for definitions ("What do we mean by *patience*?"), examples, or personal experiences related to, for example, *patience* or *impatience*.

Explain that "We are going to think about what happens as a result of bad manners and good manners. We are going to think about other people's feelings and other things that happen when we use bad manners and when we use good manners."

Explain that "The problem will begin with 'What would happen if . . . ?', and you can use your imagination to think about what happens when people either use bad manners or good manners."

As always, stress *rights of others* (and ones' own rights); elicit *empathy* ("How does it feel when . . ."); and elicit *commitments* to constructive values and behavior ("Are you the kind of person who will . . .")

As mentioned several times in this book, "What would happen if . . . ?" ideas may be stimulated by suggesting contexts: At home? In your neighborhood? In the classroom? In shopping centers and stores? On the bus? And so on. Also, watch for exercises that might be used together.

Follow-Up

Some follow-up questions are suggested after most of the problems.

"What Would Happen If . . . ?" Problems About Manners

ASKING

Problem 36.1 **What would happen if nobody ever bothered to ask before they took something?** Everyone just grabs what they want or takes what they want. Maybe your brother wants to borrow your cassette or sweatshirt, but he doesn't ask. He just takes it. Or at school someone wants to borrow your calculator, and the person just grabs it out of your desk (locker) without asking. What would happen if nobody ever bothered to ask?

Is it fair to people to just take their things without asking?

Do you like your things taken without being asked?

Is asking a good idea? Is it good manners to ask?

When we just grab things and take things without asking, are we respecting other people's rights?

Are you the type of person who will just grab things without asking?

WAITING, PATIENCE

Problem 36.2. **What would happen if nobody could wait their turn?** Everyone is in a great big hurry and just can't wait one minute for anything. Everyone wants to be first in line. Everyone wants to be first on the computer.

What would home be like?

What would school be like?

What would McDonald's be like?

Is it fair when someone just can't wait and won't take their turn?

Are you the kind of person who won't wait for your turn?

COURTESY, PLEASANTNESS

Problem 36.3 **What would happen if nobody were ever courteous, pleasant, or respectful?**

What would home be like?

What would school be like?

Would we all be happier if nobody were ever courteous, pleasant, or respectful?

Problem 36.4 **What would happen if everyone were always courteous, pleasant, and respectful?** Everyone is pleasant, polite, and respectful to everyone else.

What would home be like?

What would school be like?

Would we all be happier if everyone were always courteous, pleasant, and respectful?

Problem 36.5 **What would happen if everyone were always crabby and rude to everybody else?**

What would home be like?

What would school be like?

Would we like it if everyone were crabby and rude all the time?

SHARING

Problem 36.6   **What would happen if nobody ever shared anything at all?** If Joanne has all the crayons, then the rest of us can't color because she won't share. If Bill has a bag of chips, then the rest of us get to watch him eat them. He won't share either.

Is sharing a good idea?

Do we like it when people share things with us?

Do thoughtful people share?

Are you a person who shares things?

BEHAVING WELL IN PUBLIC

Problem 36.7   **What would happen if everybody always misbehaved in public?** Everyone tries to be loud and to annoy other people. Everybody bumps into everybody else. Everybody messes up store shelves, tries to be a loud nuisance on every bus, and crowds in front of you at the movie ticket line. What would happen?

Would we all be happier?

When children and teenagers misbehave in public, are they showing respect for other people's rights?

What do you think of people who misbehave and ignore others' rights in public?

Are you a nuisance in public?

Do YOU misbehave in public?

Problem 36.8   **What would happen if everyone always behaved well in public?** No one disturbs anyone else. No one bangs into you. No one messes up store shelves. No one crowds in lines. Everyone is polite, takes turns, and is pleasant. What would happen?

Would we all be happier?

Would we be showing respect for others' rights?

RESPECTING THE ELDERLY, PERSONS WITH DISABILITIES

Problem 36.9   **What would happen if nobody ever thought about the feelings and needs of elderly people?** If they are lonely, cold, sick, or hungry, that's just too bad. If they are robbed, maybe beaten, that's just too bad, too. What would happen if nobody every thought about the feelings and needs of elderly people?

Should we be concerned about elderly people? Why?

Do they have a right to be comfortable and treated well?

Do thoughtful people care about the safety and welfare of the elderly?

Should WE care about the safety and welfare of elderly people?

Problem 36.10 **What would happen if everyone were always rude and inconsiderate to the elderly?** No one gives them a seat on the bus. No one helps them with heavy chores.

Would that be cruel?

Do the elderly have rights? What are their rights?

Should we be helpful and polite to the elderly?

Problem 36.11 **What would happen if everyone treated the elderly with kindness and respect?**

Would the elderly be happier?

Would we feel better about ourselves?

Is it a good idea to be kind, respectful, and helpful to elderly people?

Problem 36.12 **What would happen if everyone were always rude to all persons with disabilities?**

Would the persons with disabilities be happier?

Would they be treated fairly?

Would their rights be respected?

Would the world be a better place?

What would YOU be like if you treated senior citizens badly?

Problem 36.13 **What would happen if everyone were always pleasant, helpful, and kind to persons with disabilities?** We hold open doors for people in wheelchairs. We help kids learn who have learning problems. We make sure that children who can't see well or hear well have the equipment that they need so they can learn.

Would they be happier?

Would they be treated fairly?

Would their rights be respected?

What do we think of people who are pleasant and kind to persons with disabilities? Are they thoughtful?

Should we be pleasant and helpful to persons with disabilities?

DOING FAVORS

Problem 36.14 **What would happen if nobody EVER did anyone else a favor?** If you need help carrying something heavy, that's too bad! If you need to borrow a pencil, forget it! Nobody helps anybody! What would happen?

What would school be like?

What would home be like?

What would YOU be like?

Problem 36.14 **What would happen if we always tried to do favors for people?** If we see that someone needs help, we help them.

What would school be like?

What would home be like?

What would YOU be like? Would you be a better person?

Should we help people?

Should we do favors for people?

37

Brainstorming and Reverse Brainstorming About Manners

Objectives

To increase understanding of and commitment to a few basic manners.

Time Required

Probably 5 to 15 minutes.

Getting Started

If needed, probe for (and explain) the meaning of the particular manners concept: "What do we mean by *patience, (being courteous, sharing, behaving properly in public, doing favors, . . .)*?" Explain that we are going to think about (that manners topic) by using brainstorming (or reverse brainstorming).

Review brainstorming rules: "We will think of all the ideas we can; we want a long list of ideas. We won't criticize each other's ideas, because criticism is like punishment."

With Reverse Brainstorming, remind children that "With Reverse Brainstorming, we turn the problem around. We think of how to make something WORSE. Reverse Brainstorming will help us understand how some bad manners hurt others and are bad for ourselves, and how good manners and pleasantness are better for everyone."

Prod children for additional ideas: "Anyone else have an idea?" "Jackie, do you have an idea or two?" "What about at home? In the neighborhood? At school? At the shopping center? On the bus?"

As always in brainstorming, record ideas on a chalkboard.

A teacher may use a large-group or small-group format.

Brainstorming and Reverse Brainstorming Problems

[Reverse Brainstorming problems are marked with "(R)."]

ASKING

Problem 37.1   Instead of asking permission, how many things can we just take or grab without asking the owner? List all the ideas you can. (R)

Do we like it when people take our things without asking?

Should we take someone's things without asking them?

WAITING, PATIENCE

Problem 37.2   **How many places can you think of where we just have to wait sometimes?** And it doesn't do us any good to be in a big hurry or be impatient. Where do we just have to use good manners and wait our turn?

What do we think of people who get angry or crowd in lines because they just can't wait like the rest of us? Are they showing respect for other people's rights?

Sometimes, do we just have to be patient and wait our turn?

COURTESY AND PLEASANTNESS

Problem 37.3   **How can we be VERY rude and discourteous at home?** At dinner time? In the morning? While watching TV? (R)

Does it make everyone at home happy when we are rude and discourteous?

Do we like our family to be rude and discourteous to us?

Should we be rude and discourteous to our family?

Problem 37.4   **How can we be helpful and courteous at home?** At dinner time? In the morning?

> Does it make our family happy when we are helpful and courteous?
>
> Do we like people to be helpful and courteous to us?

Problem 37.5   **How can we be VERY rude and discourteous at school?** How can we show bad manners in our classroom? (R)

Problem 37.6   **How can we show courtesy and thoughtfulness in our classroom?**

> Which do we like better, being thoughtful, helpful, and courteous? Or being rude and discourteous?

Problem 37.7   **What happens when we are discourteous or unpleasant with friends, teachers, or family members?**

> Do they like us better? Do they think we are swell people?
>
> Is it better to be courteous, pleasant, and helpful?
>
> *Should we be thoughtful, helpful, and courteous?*

SHARING

Problem 37.8   **How many things can you think of that it is nice to share?** (Treats, crayons, calculators or computers, . . .)

> Do we like it when people share things with us?
>
> *Should we share?*

Problem 37.9   **How many ways can you hurt somebody's feelings by not sharing?** (R)

> Is sharing a good idea?

BEHAVING PROPERLY IN PUBLIC

Problem 37.10   **How many ways can you think of to be real obnoxious in public, like in a shopping center or on a bus?** How can we be real rude and upset people? (R)

> What do we think of people who are loud, discourteous, and obnoxious in public? Do we admire them a lot? Do we think they are intelligent and thoughtful?

Problem 37.11   **How many ways can we be pleasant, polite, and use good manners in public, like in a shopping center or on a bus?**

What do we think of people who are pleasant, polite, and use good manners in public? Do we think they are pretty smart people?

Should we use good manners in public? Or should we be loud, rude, and obnoxious?

RESPECTING THE ELDERLY, PERSONS WITH DISABILITIES

Problem 37.12 **If we wanted to, how could we be discourteous and rude to elderly people? In stores? On buses? (R)**

Is it a good idea to be rude or discourteous with elderly people?

Does it make them happy?

Does it make them think you are a wonderful person?

Problem 37.13 **How can we show courtesy and friendliness to the elderly?**

Does it make them happy when people are friendly and courteous?

Should we be courteous and friendly with senior citizens?

Problem 37.14 **How can we show courtesy, friendliness, and helpfulness to children or adults who have disabilities?**

Is this a good idea?

Does nice treatment make them happy?

Are thoughtful people (with good values) helpful and friendly to persons with disabilities?

DOING FAVORS

Problem 37.15 **How can we do favors for each other or help each other at home?**

Do we like it when people do favors for us?

Do we like it when people are helpful?

Problem 37.16 **How can we do favors for each other or help each other in our classroom?**

Does it make us feel good to do favors for others?

Do we like it when people do favors for us?

Should we do favors for people and help people?

Chapter

38

Analogical Thinking:

"How Are Bad Manners Like a Rattlesnake?"

Objectives

To use analogies to help children think about and make decisions and commitments regarding aspects of manners.

Time Required

Often just a minute or two, perhaps a few seconds. Be ready with additional analogy problems, a follow-up discussion to clarify the analogical connection, or another activity. Do not permit a thinking session to end too quickly—encourage children to "dig a little deeper" for analogical comparisons.

Getting Started

Remind children of the meaning of "analogy": It's thinking about how things are alike. Use examples; ask children for examples. (Chalk is like a pencil; a snake is like a piece of rope; having good friends is like having wealth.)

Explain that "we are going use analogies to help us think about good manners and bad manners." Encourage children to think of as many comparisons as they can. If someone makes an analogical comparison that is unclear, explain the comparison or ask the child to do so.

Record ideas on the chalkboard.

In the classroom, a small-group format can be used. Children can be given two or three minutes (or more) to think of at least one analogy, which is then reported to the class. Groups may work on the same analogy or different ones.

Analogy Problems About Manners

Problem 38.1	How are bad manners like a rattlesnake?
Problem 38.2	How are pleasantness and good manners like a million dollars in the bank?
Problem 38.3	How are good manners like a good back rub?
Problem 38.4	How are good manners like an eagle?
Problem 38.5	How is taking something without asking like a hungry fox in the chicken coop?
Problem 38.6	How is asking (not just taking) like a beautiful rainbow?
Problem 38.7	How is sharing like Saturday?
Problem 38.8	How is being impatient and not willing to wait your turn like a bicycle with flat tires?
Problem 38.9	How is doing favors like going to the beach?
Problem 38.10	How is doing favors like giving someone money?
Problem 38.11	How is being courteous like a good vacation?
Problem 38.12	How is being courteous like sharing a candy bar?
Problem 38.13	Imagine you have a disability. Perhaps you cannot see very well or have trouble reading. How are rude classmates like a broken arcade game?
Problem 38.14	Imagine you have a disability. Perhaps you cannot hear very well or cannot do math problems. How are helpful classmates like a new puppy?

Problem 38.15   How is being rude and unpleasant at home like spending the day in an old, old garbage can?

Problem 38.16   How is being rude and inconsiderate in public like a bad automobile accident?

Taking Another Perspective:
"Would You Like To Be Brenda Bigmouth?"

Objectives

To give students practice having empathy, especially for victims of bad manners.

Time Required

These short guided discussion episodes may elicit just a few answers or many relevant ideas, experiences, perceptions, and feelings.

Getting Started

Remind children of the importance of trying to see things from others' points of view, trying to understand others' feelings. "*Having empathy* means putting yourself in someone else's shoes and understanding their thoughts and feelings. We're going to practice having empathy. Be sure to try hard to 'get into the other person's shoes' and to imagine their thoughts and feelings."

Follow-Up

Each exercise includes its own follow-up suggestions. Impromptu "What would happen if . . . ?" questions might encourage additional empathy. For example, "What would happen if nobody asked before borrowing things? If everyone were impatient? If no one were courteous and pleasant? If everyone were loud, pushy, and rude in public? If nobody ever did favors for anyone?" Problem solving, as a follow-up activity, also may stimulate thought and understanding: "What is the problem here?" and "How can we solve it?"

Taking Other Perspectives On Manners

ASKING TO BORROW THINGS

Scenario 39.1. Greta Grabber

Greta Grabber takes things without asking. In school, if she needs a pen or a pencil she just takes the first one she sees, even if it's in YOUR desk. She also helps herself to YOUR erasers and paper supplies. At home, if she wants to wear one of her sister's sweaters, she just takes it without asking. Today she borrowed her mother's sun glasses without asking. Her mom spent an hour looking for them.

How do you feel when people like Greta take things without asking?

How do Greta's friends and family feel when Greta's does this?

Is it fair to just take other people's things without asking?

Should Greta change her ways? Should Greta ASK before she just grabs things?

Should you be like Greta Grabber?

Scenario 39.2. Nateesha Always Asks

Nateesha just seems to understand that it's not right to take things without asking. So Nateesha always asks. "Mom, can I have one of your chocolates?" "Hey Shalena, can I borrow your Grateful Dead tape?" "Denzel, do you have an extra pencil? I'll give it back right after school."

What does Nateesha's mother and Nateesha's friends think about her habit of asking, not grabbing? Do they think she is trustworthy?

What do you think? Do you like people to ask? Or to just grab?

Should YOU be like Nateesha, and always ask before taking something?

WAITING, PATIENCE

Scenario 39.3. **Line-Crashing Teenagers**

Imagine you are in front of a movie theater. You are waiting in line to buy a ticket. You see three teenagers walk right up to the front of the line, step in front of an elderly lady, buy their tickets and walk in.

What do you think about this? It is right?

What does the elderly lady think of these teenagers?

Were the teenagers thinking about other people's rights and feelings?

Is it fair for people to crowd in line?

Should everyone wait their turn?

Would you crowd in line or wait your turn?

COURTESY, PLEASANTNESS, BEHAVING PROPERLY IN PUBLIC

Scenario 39.4. **Brenda Bigmouth**

Brenda Bigmouth is a rude person. She knocks people out of the way on the street. She yells at tourists to "Go back where you came from!" She snaps at store clerks who don't do exactly what she wants. She even knocks things onto the floor, deliberately. Her own mother is afraid to talk to her, because Brenda swears at her and yells insults at her.

If you were a tourist what would you think of Brenda?

What do store clerks think of Brenda?

Does Brenda think about other people's feelings?

What do you think of Brenda?

Would you like Brenda for a friend?

Would you like to be Brenda?

Scenario 39.5. **Cordial Carla**

Believe it or not, Carla is Brenda's sister. Carla doesn't know why Brenda is such a grouchy, difficult person. Carla tries to be the exact opposite. When she sees tourists on the street, she'll say "Welcome to Cedar City! I hope you're having a nice vacation!" She is patient and pleasant in stores. She even puts things back on the shelves when they get knocked off. Carla and her mother respect each others' rights, treat each other well, and they get along great!

What does Carla know that Brenda doesn't?

Would Carla probably be a better friend than Brenda?

Should everyone be more like Carla than Brenda?

Should you be more like Carla than Brenda?

SHARING

Scenario 39.6. **Charlie and the Chocolates**

Little Charlie is sitting in his third-grade classroom before the afternoon session begins. Three children walk in with some bags of *M & M's*—yummy chocolate covered peanuts. They ignore Charlie. They don't offer him any of their *M & M's*.

How does Charlie feel?

Why didn't the three students share?

Did they think about Charlie's feelings?

Should they share their candy with Charlie? Why?

Would they feel good if their shared with Charlie?

Is sharing a good idea?

Scenario 39.7. **Shonita Shares**

Little Charlie once again is sitting in his third-grade classroom before the afternoon session begins. Shonita walks in with a small bag of potato chips—chive and sour cream flavored! She looks at Charlie. Charlie looks at Shonita. Shonita smiles and says, "Hey Charlie, you look hungry. Have some chips. Better hurry before class starts!" Charlie grins all over!

How does Charlie feel?

How does Shonita feel?

Is sharing a good thing to do?

RESPECTING THE ELDERLY, PERSONS WITH DISABILITIES

Scenario 39.8. **Mrs. Adeline Smith, Age 80**

Mrs. Adeline Smith is 80 years old. She is small and weak, doesn't have much money, and lives alone. In front of the grocery store, rowdy teenagers deliberately stand in her way. She has to walk around them. Then they yell, "Look at the old fogey!"

How do you think Mrs. Smith feel about this? Is she frightened? Does she feel helpless?

What does she think of these teenagers?

Do the teenagers think about Mrs. Smith's feelings?

Do the teenagers think about Mrs. Smith's rights?

Would you like to be Mrs. Smith? (Some day, you might be Mrs. Smith or Mr. Smith.)

Would you ever be rude and impolite to an elderly person?

Scenario 39.9. Lavonzelle Is Helpful

Lavonzelle is in the fourth grade. She lives next door to Mr. Angelo, who is 84 years old and lives alone. Lavonzelle always smiles and says "Hi Mr. Angelo!" If he needs help with something, Lavonzelle is quick to give him a hand. Maybe carrying something or holding the door for him. Mr. Angelo likes Lavonzelle a LOT.

Do we earn respect and friendship by helping others?

Is it a good idea to be friendly and helpful with the elderly?

Should we all be friendly and helpful with our elderly neighbors?

Scenario 39.10. Fred's in a Wheelchair

Fred Johansen is in a wheelchair. He is a nice, friendly, intelligent boy. But in class, students seem afraid of him. They don't talk to him. They don't invite him to parties. Sometimes Fred feels invisible. Some rude students deliberately bump his wheelchair, slam the door on him, and even call him names.

How do you think Fred feels about being ignored?

How does Fred feel about being treated rudely?

What does Fred think of the rude students? Does he think they are swell people?

What do YOU think of the rude students?

Do persons with disabilities have a right to be treated in a friendly way? To be helped, if necessary?

If you were in a wheelchair, would you want people to talk to you and be friendly?

Scenario 39.11. Nancy Has Diabetes

Nancy has diabetes. She can't see very well and is weak. EVERYBODY in the class is friendly with Nancy. Everybody tries to help her. They take turns reading the lessons to her. They work with her on math problems. They are friends with Nancy outside of school, too. Nancy is doing fine in school and really likes her classmates.

How does Nancy feel about the good treatment by her friends?

Do persons with disabilities deserve to be treated in friendly ways and to be helped, when they need help?

Should we be friends with students with disabilities?

BEHAVING PROPERLY IN PUBLIC

Scenario 39.12. You Are a "Stop-And-Go" Cashier

Imagine you are a cashier in a small "Stop-And-Go" store. Every day at noon, six teenagers come in. They yell and swear, mess up your magazine rack, bump into people, throw papers on the floor, and you suspect that they steal candy bars and other things.

As the cashier, how do you feel about these students? Do you like them?

Do you like to clean up after them?

Do they see themselves from your point of view?

Should they think about your rights and feelings?

Visualization:

"Imagine You're a Big, Dumb, Pushy Bully!"

Objectives

Strengthening empathy—the ability to understand others' thoughts, feelings, and perspectives.

Time Required

Introductions and narrations require about 10 minutes. The follow-up discussion of perceptions and feelings may require another 5 or 10 minutes.

Getting Started

Remind children of the importance of understanding other people's thoughts, feelings, and points of view. Remind them that we will be less likely to hurt or mistreat others if we can think about what it is like to be hurt or mistreated.

Have everyone "Get comfortable, shut your eyes, and imagine what is happening in your 'mind's eye.' Be sure to try to understand the feelings and the thoughts of the people involved." Read or paraphrase the scenarios fairly slowly, with pauses as indicated by ellipses (. . .).

Follow-Up

Each scenario includes its own follow-up questions. Help clarify the feelings and perceptions so that all students understand the problem (or the good behavior) from the point of the view of persons involved.

Try to elicit commitment to the idea that "This behavior (manners, value) is bad (wrong) because it hurts other people and it hurts ourselves," or "This behavior (value) is helpful to others."

A problem solving approach can be a good follow-up: "What is the problem here?" and "How can we solve it?"

Visualization Activities: Manners

RUDENESS, NAME CALLING, ATROCIOUS CLASSROOM BEHAVIOR

Scenario 40.1. **You're a Big Dumb, Pushy Bully**

Imagine that you are a big dumb, pushy bully named Bobby . . . It's Monday morning and you are walking down the school hall . . . You see a smaller child and you yell, "Hey stupid, is that your face or a pile of garbage?" . . . The little child is startled and becomes upset . . . You laugh because you think you are funny . . . You think to yourself, "It's fun to yell at little kids and call them names . . . They wouldn't DARE yell back at ME! . . .

In class, your teacher, Ms. Ruiz, asks you, "Bobby, which is the third planet from the sun?" . . . You say, "Uh, how should I know? I ain't never been there!" . . . Then you turn to Maggie in the next seat and whisper, "Hey Lanky, how come you're so tall an' skinny? Weather okay up there? Glad I ain't a toothpick like you!" . . . Then you look at Ms. Ruiz and yell, "Hey Ruiz, ain't it time fer art yet?" . . . The teacher replies, "My name is Ms. Ruiz, Bobby. And you know it's not time for art yet . . . And where are your manners? We don't yell at each other in this class." . . .

Finally it is art time . . . While everyone waits for the art teacher to arrive, you walk to the front of the room and grab the best set of water colors . . . It has Maggie's name on it . . . The art teacher arrives. She sees you take Maggie's paints . . . "Bobby, if you want a different set of paints, please try asking" . . . You mumble, "Uh, but I need THIS one. That toothpick don't want it" . . . After art class, you look at another student and laugh out loud, "Hey, you're as ugly as a horse!" . . .

Well, Bobby, do you think other people like to be yelled at? Called names?

Do you like people to yell at you? Insult you? Treat you rudely? Call you names? Why not?

How does it feel to be yelled at, treated rudely, or be called names? Is it a good feeling?

What do you think about people like Bobby? Are they considerate? Thoughtful? Intelligent?

Should you REALLY be like Bobby?

Are you someone who could be like Bobby?

WAITING, PATIENCE, COURTESY, BEHAVING PROPERLY IN PUBLIC, BEING CONSIDERATE WITH ELDERLY

Scenario 40.2. Jan Is Always Impatient

Jan is always impatient . . . Today is Saturday . . . She came into the kitchen and said to her mom, "I'd like some pancakes for breakfast—can you hurry as fast as you can, I need to get going!" . . . She grabbed her brother's plate and took his glass of milk . . . "He isn't here yet," Jan thought to herself . . . "Besides, it's too much trouble to get my own . . ." "Mom, can you hurry with breakfast?" . . .

Later at the department store some people were waiting in line to pay for their things . . . Jan stepped in at the front and shoved her money at the clerk . . . "I don't have to wait if I don't want to," she thought to herself . . . Jan did the same thing at a popcorn stand . . . She popped right in front of people who had been waiting and loudly ordered a soda and a bag of popcorn . . . And once more at the bus stop, she just crowded in front of everyone else and grabbed a seat by a window . . . The bus was getting full . . . An elderly man with a cane was standing near Jan . . . "I don't see him," she laughed to herself . . . A little later she almost knocked him down, because she wanted to be the first one off the bus . . . Jan was sure in a hurry . . .

Should we demand that other people "hurry up" just because we don't feel like waiting? Is this fair to them?

How do you feel when people crowd in front of you when you are waiting in line?

Is it fair to push ahead of others?

If you were the elderly man with the cane on the bus, what would you think about Jan's bus manners? Is she considerate and polite?

Should we wait our turn, be pleasant, not rush our mom, and be polite to senior citizens (and give them our seat on the bus)?

Or should we be like Jan?

SHARING, BEING PLEASANT

Scenario 40.3.   Sharing and Pleasantness Lessons From Pat

Imagine that your name is Pat . . . You like being a kind, thoughtful, sharing person . . . And you want other people to think of you as a kind, thoughtful, sharing person . . . It is your birthday and your sister gives you a beautiful box of chocolates . . . You thank her, open the box, and let her have first choice . . . She picks out a chocolate covered peanut cluster and smiles from ear to ear . . . Your aunt and uncle stop by to wish you happy birthday . . . They give you $5 and a birthday card . . . You smile and thank them and offer them some chocolates . . . They say, "How wonderful, I love chocolates. That's very nice of you!" . . . You hear them tell your mother, "Pat is certainly a nice person. So many kids these days have bad manners" . . .

A little later you are about to leave the house, but you notice mom clearing the dishes off the table . . . You ask yourself, "Should I leave? Or should I help mom for a few minutes?" . . . You know the answer . . . You help mom clear the table and get the dishes done . . . It only took about five minutes . . . She smiles says, "Thanks a lot Pat. Have a happy birthday!" . . . As you leave, your neighbor, Mrs. Cortez, waves from her porch and calls, "Happy birthday, Pat!" . . . You jog over, take the lid of your precious box of chocolates and offer her one . . . You feel very good about sharing and being nice to people . . .

How do you feel when you share things and help people? Good? Happy?

How do you feel when people share things with you? Good? Happy?

Is it fun to make people happy by sharing?

Are you the kind of person who shares things?

41

Questions and Discussion About Manners

Objectives

To increase awareness of and commitments to values related to some elementary manners.

Time Required

If an issue is relatively simple, a few minutes (or seconds) may adequately cover a discussion. Ten minutes or more might be spent on interrelated questions. More time would be needed if the teacher or parent follows up with an impromptu brainstorming or "What would happen if . . . ?" problem.

Getting Started

Orient students to the purpose of the discussion. "We're going to think about how important it is to use good manners—to be pleasant, polite, and thoughtful with others. Just like we want others to be pleasant, polite, and thoughtful with us."

Discussion Questions

ASKING

41.1   If someone has something you would like to borrow, such as a pencil or a calculator, should you ask to use it or just grab it? Why?

41.2   What do you think when someone takes something of yours without asking?

41.3   Are you the kind of person who just grabs things without asking?

WAITING, PATIENCE

41.4   Imagine you are standing in line in the school cafeteria. Joe and Nancy walk to the front of the line, step in front of everyone, and get their lunches. Is this right? Is it fair? Why not?

41.5   What do we think of people who push ahead of us when we're waiting in line somewhere—maybe in the cafeteria or at a movie theater. Are they considerate? Thoughtful? Fair-minded? Bad-mannered? Do they think about other people's rights or feelings?

COURTESY, PLEASANTNESS, RUDENESS, NAME-CALLING

41.6   What is "courtesy"?

41.7   What is the opposite of being courteous? (Being rude? Ill-mannered? Unpleasant? Thoughtless?)

41.8   What are some examples of being courteous?

41.9   What are some examples of being discourteous?

41.10 What do we think of discourteous, rude, unpleasant people?

41.11 Which is best, being courteous or being discourteous?

41.12 Is it enjoyable when someone calls you names? Is that a lot of fun?

41.13 How do we feel when people call us names? Sad? Hurt? Angry?

41.14 What would you think if I said "Hey, stupid!" or "Hey, dummy!", instead of "Terrell" or "Jennifer"? Or if I said "Look at that dumb Jackie, what a stupid ribbon she's wearing!" Would you think I was an intelligent, pleasant, considerate person?

41.15 Do intelligent, considerate people call other people names whenever they feel like it?

41.16 What do we think of people who are always calling other people names? (Are they the "jerks"?)

SHARING

41.17 How do you feel when someone has some candy, cookies, or potato chips and they DON'T share them with you? (A little upset? Hurt?) Are they being polite and thoughtful?

41.18 Is sharing a good idea? Do we make people happy when we share?

41.19 What do we think of people who share?

BEHAVING WELL IN PUBLIC

41.20 Imagine you are in a department store. You see some teenagers yelling, laughing loudly, and messing up stacks of shirts and sweaters. Should they do that? What do you think of them?

41.21 Imagine YOU are the teenagers that are doing the yelling and messing. Do you really want people to think you are stupid, inconsiderate, and bad mannered? (They will!)

41.22 What is proper behavior in any public place? (Being polite? Respecting others rights? Not leaving messes? Not yelling or playing your boom box?)

41.23 When we are in public places, should we think about how we look to other people? Will that help us figure out what we ought to do? How we ought to behave? Do we want to look like rude, bad-mannered idiots?

41.24 Can we imagine that WE are the people who are being treated rudely or discourteously? Can we imagine that WE are the people who are being bothered by yelling and noise? Will that help us figure out how we ought to behave?

RESPECT FOR THE ELDERLY, PERSONS WITH DISABILITIES

41.25 Should we be courteous and considerate with elderly people? Why?

41.26 Have you heard of cases where elderly people have been beaten and robbed?

41.27 Why does that happen? Is it fair? Is it right?

41.28 What sort of people do that? Do they to think about the rights and feelings of the elderly?

41.29   Do elderly people deserve respect and dignity?

41.30   Should we be courteous, pleasant, and helpful with people who have disabilities? Why?

41.31   Imagine that you have no legs, and so you are in a wheelchair. Are you still a normal, friendly person? Do you still want friends? Do you still want people to say "hello" to you? Do you still want people to talk to you at lunch?

DOING FAVORS

41.32   Is it a good idea to do favors for people? Why?

41.33   How do we feel when we help someone? Good?

41.34   How do we feel when someone helps us? Good?

41.35   Is it right to see people who need a little help, and NOT help them if we can? (Maybe they're loaded with packages and they drop something. Or maybe they need help with a door.)

GENERAL

41.36   Do we want to be someone who is respected by others? Do we want to respect ourselves? Or is it all right to be a dishonest, irresponsible, unfair, messy, rude person with horrible manners whom nobody likes very much?

41.37   Can we promise ourselves to be pleasant, fair, and respect others' rights?

41.38   Do we like others to use good manners around us? Should we use good manners?

41.39   Will we be better off in our lives if we try to be pleasant, fair, and respect others' rights? If we try to use good manners at home, in school, and in public?

Word Search and Crossword Puzzles About Manners

Two word search puzzles
and one crossword puzzle
involve manners-related
words. The puzzles are on
separate pages so you may
copy and use them without
trashing the book. Solutions
are at the end of the
chapter.

Word Search for GOOD MANNERS Words

In this puzzle you can search for words related to good manners. These words show others that you care about their rights. And that you are a smart and thoughtful person.

The words are printed left to right or top to bottom. One word is printed from right to left (backwards).

Find these words and draw a ring around them.

Manners	Polite	Patience	Favors
Sharing	Taking Turns	Helpful	Respectful
Asking	Courteous		

```
T M A N N E R S Q
A S K I N G E Z C
K C P X H K S U O
I V A K E Y P B U
N R T Z L N E Y R
G R I T P I C F T
T G E W F Z T A E
U X N R U P F V O
R D C X L M U O U
N M E T O X L R S
S H A R I N G S Q
L J K E T I L O P
```

Word Search For BAD MANNERS Words

This is a word search puzzle about BAD manners. These words are about things that hurt others. They are about violating others' rights. If you do these things, people will think you are not a very nice person. The words are printed left to right or top to bottom. One word is printed from right to left (backwards).

Find these words and draw a ring around them.

Impolite	Mean	Not Asking	Yelling
Pushy	Noisy	Unpleasant	Grabbing
Rude	Name Calling		

```
E D U R X N P U S H Y
K U N O T A S K I N G
W F P F Q M P Q Y Z R
I K L T M E A N D K A
M W E S K C X N D L B
P M A O Z A Z O C Q B
O Y S Y E L L I N G I
L Z A B Y L X S J D N
I J N Z R I L Y M X G
T W T C K N R H W K B
E M N X V G F E D U R
```

From *Teaching Values* published by Westwood Publishing Co. © 1996 Gary A. Davis

Crossword Puzzle: Manners Words

Most of the words in this crossword puzzle are about manners. But some words don't have anything to do with anything.

Write the answers in the "checkerboard," with one letter in each square. Start each answer in the square that has the same number as the question.

Write "Across" words in the regular way, from left to right.

Write "Down" words from top to bottom (vertically).

ACROSS

1. When teenagers commit crimes and go to jail, some adults ask, "_____'s wrong with our kids these days?"

4. There are good manners and there are _____ manners.

6. Tawana gave Latricia some popcorn. Tawana was _____ her popcorn.

8. Some kids are polite and well-behaved in public. They take turns, share, and are respectful to adults. They have good _____.

10. Opposite of "hers."

12. Joe tries to use good manners. Joe tries to be _____. (Rhymes with *go right*.)

13. First you ride a _____-cycle, then a bicycle.

15. Children who are bullies, rude, and noisy in public and call people names and take things without asking are acting really _____. (Rhymes with *cupid*.)

19. Juan shoves little kids around, threatens them, and takes their lunch money. Juan is a _____. (Not *jerk* or *creep*, but you are close; it rhymes with *woolly*.)

20. Initials of New Orleans; and you say it to drugs.

DOWN

1. Sometimes we can't rush; sometimes we must _____.

2. We should _____ before we take things.

3. It helps people, and it make us feel good, when we do people _____. (Rhymes with *flavors*.)

4. Abbreviation for "body odor."

5. It shows we have good manners when we hold open _____ for people.

7. Leon never asks. If he wants something, he will just _____ it. (Rhymes with *crab*.)

9. _____-calling is rude and hurtful.

10. It is not good manners to _____ senior citizens over the head with chairs.

11. In public, Susan yells, swears, and blasts her boom box. Susan makes a lot of noise; she is really _____. (Rhymes with *boys see*.)

14. "Good mannered" is better than "_____-mannered."

16. Pleasant is better than _____-pleasant.

17. Abbreviation for "Post Office."

18. Donald Duck's initials.

From *Teaching Values* published by Westwood Publishing Co. © 1996 Gary A. Davis

Solutions to Puzzles in This Chapter

Word Search for GOOD MANNERS Words

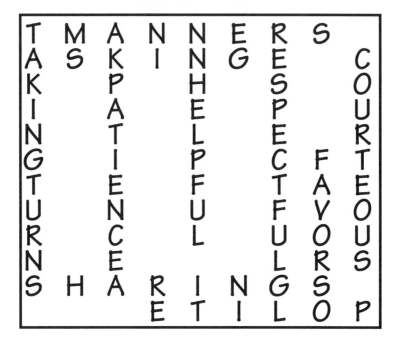

Word Search for BAD MANNERS Words

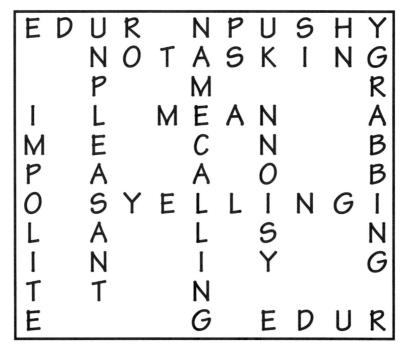

(Yes, RUDE is in two places.)

Crossword Puzzle

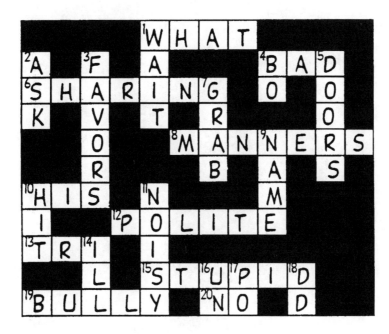

Part VII

Valuing Education, School and Work Habits

C h a p t e r

43

"What Would Happen If ...

Nobody Went to School?"

What Is "Valuing Education, School and Work Habits"?

The topic of "Valuing Education, School And Work Habits" is both narrow and broad. It includes small issues, such as paying attention and doing neat work, and larger ones that appeared in earlier chapters, for example, achievement motivation and the critical lifetime importance of education and job training. This section will focus on the following values:

Valuing Education   Achievement Motivation, Self-Motivation

Paying Attention   Promptness

Doing a Good Job   Using Time Wisely (Well)

Doing Neat Work   Observing Safety Rules

Understanding Purposes of Rules

Accepting Leadership and Followership Roles

Objectives

In this chapter, each "What Would Happen If . . . ?" problem tries to increase awareness, understanding, and commitment to constructive values related to valuing education and school and work habits.

Time Required

Three to 10 minutes per activity, depending upon the problem and student interest, plus time for introductions and follow-ups.

Getting Started

If needed, discuss the meaning of the particular focus topic (e.g., *promptness, using time wisely, followership*). You might ask for definitions ("What do we mean by *using time wisely/well*?") or examples ("Where do we see people *using their time wisely/well*?).

Explain that "We are going to think about what happens as a result of (e.g., being a good listener, being a good follower, etc.). Explain that "The problem will begin with 'What would happen if . . . ?' and you can use your imagination to think about what happens when people (e.g., listen carefully to directions, don't listen carefully to directions)."

As always, try to elicit *commitments* to constructive values and behavior: "Are you the kind of person who will help (hurt) yourself by . . . ."

"What Would Happen If . . . ?" Problems

PAYING ATTENTION

Problem 43.1   **What would happen if nobody ever listened to directions?** In school? At home? Adults at work?

Would we know what to do?

Would we be able to do a good job?

Problem 43.2   **What would happen if we all paid CAREFUL attention when we are asked to do things?** So we all know exactly what we are supposed to do.

Would our work be easier?

Can we do a better job that way?

Is listening carefully to directions a good idea?

PROMPTNESS

Problem 43.3   **What would happen if everybody were always late?** Nobody is ever on time for school. Everybody is late for work. Everybody is late for our appointments with the doctor or dentist. Everybody is late to catch their train or plane. What would happen?

Would the teacher be able to teach?

Does it interrupt our work when children come to class late?

Would workers probably lose their jobs?

Would we miss our buses, trains, and planes if we were always late?

Would doctors and dentists be able to do their jobs if everyone were late?

Problem 43.4 **What would happen if everyone were ON TIME or even EARLY for school, for work, at the doctor's office, or at the bus stop or train station?**

Would things run more smoothly?

Would we be better off being on time rather than late?

ACHIEVEMENT MOTIVATION, USING TIME WELL

Problem 43.5 **What would happen if everyone were lazy?** Everyone wastes time. Nobody has any motivation. Nobody does things they are supposed to do. Nobody cares whether they finish their work or not. Nobody tries to do a good job? Everyone just daydreams in school or watches TV all day at home.

What would we all be like?

What would you be like?

What would you be like when you grow up?

Problem 43.6 **What would happen if everyone liked to work hard?** Everyone gets their jobs done. Everyone tries to do a good job. Everyone sets their goals and goes after them!

Would we be more successful?

Would we be proud of our accomplishments?

Would we probably be happier when we are adults?

Which is better, being lazy and wasting time? Or working hard and doing a good job?

Problem 43.7 **What would happen if nobody ever tried to do a good job?** Your dentist does sloppy work. Your mom or dad don't try to do a good job at work. Your teacher doesn't care if you learn anything. What would happen?

Would people be proud of their sloppy work?

Would their jobs get done well?

Is it best to try to do careful work?

Problem 43.8   **What will happen if YOU get into the habit of doing sloppy work?**

> Would you be proud of your work?
>
> Would others be proud of your work?
>
> Is it best to try to do careful work?

Problem 43.9   **What would happen if YOU get into the habit of doing jobs really, really well—neatly, on time, and well done?**

> Would you be proud of your work?
>
> Would others be proud of your work?
>
> Is it best to try to do careful work?

LEADERSHIP, FOLLOWERSHIP

Problem 43.10   **What would happen if nobody wanted to be a leader.** Nobody wants to be responsible for getting things organized and getting things done. Nobody wants to plan the class picnic or the school play. Nobody wants to organize our recycling program. Nobody wants to plan the family vacation. Everybody just waits for someone else to do the work. What would happen?

> Would anything get done?
>
> Is it a good idea to be a leader sometimes? And make sure things get done?
>
> *Should YOU be a leader sometimes?*

Problem 43.11   **What would happen if everybody refused to be a follower?** Nobody wants to take orders from anybody else. Nobody wants to follow instructions.

> Would anything get done?
>
> Do we need to be good followers sometimes? To do what we are asked to do, and try to do a good job?

VALUING EDUCATION

Problem 43.12   **What would happen if nobody went to school?**

> Is school important? Why?

Problem 43.13   **What would happen if nobody went on to technical school or to college?** Nobody learned technical job skills or a profession.

> Is technical school or college important?

Should we try hard to graduate from high school and go on for more education and training?

Problem 43.14 **What WILL happen if we all graduate from high school, then we all go to college or a technical school for good professional training?**

Will we be able to get a good job and earn good money?

Will we be better able to have a successful, comfortable life?

Is education and training important?

Should we try hard to graduate from high school and then go to college or a technical school?

UNDERSTANDING PURPOSES OF RULES, OBEYING SAFETY RULES

Problem 43.15 **What would happen if we didn't have ANY rules in our school?** No rules about what time to be here. No rules about recess or lunch time. No rules about being nice to each another. No rules about cleaning up after ourselves. What would happen?

Do rules help us understand what to do? When to do it?

Do rules help things to run smoothly?

Are rules important?

Should we pay attention to rules?

Should we follow rules?

Problem 43.16 **What would happen if we didn't have ANY rules at home?** We all just do what we want whenever we want to. Nobody fixes breakfast or dinner. Nobody does laundry or straightens the house. Nobody helps with anything. Nobody is ever nice to anyone else.

Do family rules help things to run smoothly?

Do family rules help us to get along better?

Are family rules important?

Problem 43.17 **What would happen if we all ignored all safety rules?** We ignore the crossing guards and walk out into traffic. We run down slippery hallways. We try all the pills and medicine at home. We taste all the washing soap and kitchen cleaning liquids we can find. We play with electrical wires. In the car we never buckle our seat belt. What would happen?

Is it a good idea to pay attention to safety rules? Why?

Brainstorming and Reverse Brainstorming:

"How Many Excuses Can We Think Of?"

Reverse brainstorming problems, especially, should be fun—thinking of excuses, thinking of ways to waste time, thinking of what to do instead of paying attention, and so on. Fun is fine. Children should get the message.

Objectives

To increase awareness and understanding of, and commitment to, values pertaining to education, school and work habits, and general achievement motivation. Many exercises overlap with values discussed in earlier sections.

Time Required

Approximately 5 to 15 minutes.

Getting Started

Be sure everyone understands the vocabulary. If needed, probe for and explain the meaning of the concepts: "What do we mean by *paying attention* (*excuses, using time wisely, wasting time, safety rules*)?"

Explain that we are going to think about (a topic) by using brainstorming (or reverse brainstorming).

Review brainstorming rules: We will think of all the ideas we can; we want a long list of ideas. We don't criticize each other's ideas.

With Reverse Brainstorming, remind children that "With Reverse Brainstorming, we turn the problem around. We think of how to make something WORSE. Reverse Brainstorming helps us understand a problem better. Reverse Brainstorming helps us understand how good values can help us live better lives and be more successful."

Prod children for additional ideas: "Anyone else have an idea?" "Terrell, do you have an idea?"

Record ideas on the chalkboard or have a volunteer do so.

A teacher may use a large-group or small-group format.

Brainstorming and Reverse Brainstorming Problems

[Reverse Brainstorming problems are marked with "(R)."]

PAYING ATTENTION

Problem 44.1 **How many things can we do instead of paying attention to the teacher?** (R)

Do we ever do these things?

Do we hear directions when we do not pay attention?

Do we know what to do if we don't listen to directions?

Does paying attention help us to be better learners?

Is paying attention a good idea?

PROMPTNESS

Problem 44.2 **How many excuses can we think of for being late for school?** (R) Use your imagination. What excuses have you heard?

What happens when we are late for school? Do we interrupt the class? Do we interrupt the teacher?

Is it a good idea to be on time?

Problem 44.3 **How many places can we think of where it is important to be on time?** (School? Getting home? Meeting friends? Catching buses? Doctor appointments? ANY time we say we will be some place at a certain time? . . .)

When somebody says they will be at your house at four o'clock, do you like them to show up at 4:30 or five o'clock?

Should we be on time? Or should we make people wait for us?

SELF-MOTIVATION

Problem 44.4   **Instead of working hard at something, what excuses can we make up to show that we would rather just give up and not even try?** (R) What are some excuses for not working hard?

Do we hurt ourselves when we make excuses for not trying? How? (Lose skills, develop bad work habit, get lazy, . . .)

Should we try hard to do a good job?

USING TIME WELL

Problem 44.5   **How many different ways can we waste time instead of using our time well?** (R) In school? At home?

Is it all right to waste time ALL the time?

Is it all right to work hard sometimes, and relax and have fun other times?

Problem 44.6   **How many different places can we think of where it is important to use our time well, and not waste it?**

In school?

Doing chores at home?

Is it all right to work hard sometimes, and relax and have fun other times?

DOING A GOOD JOB, DOING NEAT WORK

Problem 44.7   **How many different ways can you prove you are a sloppy person—a real slob?** (R) In school? At home?

Is it a good idea to be a sloppy slob? Why not?

Problem 44.8   **How many ways can we do a BAD job in our school work or doing chores at home?** (R) How can we be sure to mess things up. To not finish the job. To make people think we are lazy and irresponsible? Let's think of all the ideas we can.

Which is better for everyone, trying to do doing a good job or just doing a sloppy, incomplete, poor job?

Are we proud when we do a good job?

Problem 44.9 **How many different kinds of projects can you think of where it is important to do neat work?** In school? At home?

> Are we proud of neat work?
>
> When we get older and get a job, will it be important to do neat work? Why?

VALUING EDUCATION, ACHIEVEMENT MOTIVATION

Problem 44.10 **What happens to people when they drop out of high school?** Let's think of all of the ideas we can. (Suggesting categories may help: General level of education and knowledge? Job skills and opportunities? Getting admitted to a technical school or college? Eventual social and financial level? Security? Enjoyment of life?)

> Is this a BIG HARMFUL LIFE DECISION when teenagers decide to drop out of high school?

Problem 44.11 **How many reasons can you think of to get as much education as you can?**

> Will the education and training you get when you are young AFFECT YOUR WHOLE LIFE? Is this important?
>
> Is your decision about education and training ONE OF THE MOST IMPORTANT DECISIONS OF YOUR LIFE?
>
> *What do you think you should do?*

Problem 44.12 **How many ways can you think of to learn as little as possible in school (so you will know absolutely nothing when you graduate from high school)?** (R)

> Would you like to be an educated person? Understand your world? Be ready for further education and training?
>
> If YOU learn nothing in school, who suffers?

UNDERSTANDING RULES

Problem 44.13 **How many different rules can we think of at home?** Rules about getting up, eating, helping with meals or dishes, TV, homework, cleaning our rooms, yard work, . . .

> Are rules at home important? Why?
>
> Do rules help things run smoother?
>
> Do rules usually make our lives better?

Problem 44.14 **How many different rules can we think of at school?** For our classroom? About time schedules? About class work? About being kind to one another? About recess? About getting and returning materials?

Are rules important? Why?

Should we follow rules in order to help things move smoothly?

OBSERVING SAFETY RULES

Problem 44.15 **How many different safety rules can you think of?** (Suggest contexts: in the classroom, hallways, playgrounds, crossing streets, at home, on buses, at the swimming pool, boating, in the car, . . .)

Why do we have safety rules? (Just so adults can boss around children?)

Why should we obey safety rules?

Problem 44.16 **How many different ways can you think of to violate safety rules** (and maybe injure yourself)? (R)

Are safety rules a good idea?

Chapter

45

Analogical Thinking:

"How Is a Good Education Like a Good Dream?"

Objectives

To help children think about and make decisions and commitments regarding the value of education and training and more specific school and work habits.

Time Required

Often just a minute or two, perhaps a few seconds. Be ready with additional analogy problems, follow-up discussion to clarify the analogical connection, or another activity. But do not permit a thinking session to end too quickly—encourage children to "put on their thinking caps" and try to find more analogical connections.

Getting Started

Remind children of the meaning of "analogy": It's thinking about how things are alike. Also, be sure children understand the concept(s) at hand (e.g., *leader* versus *follower*).

Explain that "We are going use analogies to help us think about why education and training are important and how good work habits help us succeed." Encourage children to think of as many comparisons as they can. Be sure to explain, or have the child explain, unclear comparisons.

Record ideas on the chalkboard. In the classroom, a small-group format can be used. Children would be given two or three minutes (or more) to think of one or more analogies, which are then reported to the class. Groups may work on the same analogy problem or different ones.

Analogy Problems: Valuing Education and School and Work Habits

Problem 45.1	How is not paying attention like a broken toy?
Problem 45.2	How is not paying attention like having a sack over your head?
Problem 45.3	How is being late like having a bad cold?
Problem 45.4	How is being late like a race horse that stays in the barn?
Problem 45.5	How is being on time like listening to music that you like?
Problem 45.6	How is making a good effort to accomplish things like an ice cream sundae?
Problem 45.7	How is wasting time in school like a watching a really stupid TV show at home?
Problem 45.8	How is working hard and using our time well in school like a birthday cake?
Problem 45.9	How is doing neat work like being a pilot and flying an airplane?
Problem 45.10	How is messy work like a bulldozer that's gone crazy?
Problem 45.11	How are good leaders and good followers alike?
Problem 45.12	How is a good education like a good dream?
Problem 45.13	How is a good education like a free ticket to Disneyland?
Problem 45.14	How is dropping out of school like a car that won't start?
Problem 45.15	How is dropping out of school like jumping out of a plane with no parachute?

Problem 45.16 How are school rules like a good road map?

Problem 45.17 How are rules at home like a picture puzzle?

Problem 45.18 How are safety rules like parts of a computer?

Problem 45.19 How is ignoring safely rules like a cowboy riding a moose?

Taking Another Perspective:

"How Does Doran Dropout Feel?"

Objectives

To use empathy to increase children's understanding of the value of education and positive school and work habits.

Time Required

These brief guided discussion exercises may elicit just a few answers or many relevant ideas and experiences about perceptions and feelings.

Getting Started

Remind children of the importance of trying to see things from others' points of view, trying to understand others feelings. *"Having empathy means putting yourself in someone else's shoes and understanding their thoughts and feelings. We're going to practice having empathy. Be sure to try hard to 'get into the other person's shoes,' try hard to imagine their thoughts and feelings."*

Follow-Up

Each exercise includes its own follow-up suggestions. In addition, impromptu "What would happen if . . . ?" and brainstorming-type questions ("How many ways can we think of to . . .") can encourage additional understanding and commitment.

Taking Another Perspective

Scenario 46.1.   **Fickle Phil Doesn't Pay Attention**

Imagine you are Fickle Phil. You never pay attention to instructions. In school you ignore the teacher's directions, then ask your friends what you are supposed to do. At home you don't pay attention when mom explains where your clean clothes are, and so you can't find anything to wear. You just don't listen to directions!

> What happens when Fickle Phil doesn't listen to directions?
>
> How does Phil feel when he has to ask other children what the teacher said? Is he embarrassed? Does he feel kind of silly? Maybe he feels kind of dumb?
>
> Should Phil listen to instructions? Why?

Scenario 46.2   **You Are Always Late**

Imagine that you are always late—to school, to dinner, and to meet friends. You just can't seem to be on time for anything.

> How do think your friends feel about your habit of being late?
>
> What do your parents think?
>
> Are you being fair to others by making others wait for you?
>
> Are you wasting their time by making them wait for you?

Scenario 46.3   **Late For Work**

Imagine you are 16 years old and you have a new job—selling burgers and fries at Burger Queen! But you are always late for work.

> What does your boss think about your habit of being late? Does he or she like it?
>
> Is your boss likely to give you a big raise in salary?
>
> Is your boss likely to give you a promotion to a better job?
>
> Is your boss likely to give you a good recommendation to other employers?
>
> Is it fair to other workers when you are not there to help out?

Scenario 46.4   Lazy Chris

Chris Cramden is lazy—REALLY lazy. Never works any more than necessary. Never finishes anything. Never cleans anything up. Does as little as possible. Expects to be a professional nobody when out of school.

Would you like to be Chris?

When you grow up, would you like to be married to Chris?

If Chris gets a job, what will Chris's bosses think of Chris?

Will Chris keep the job long?

Scenario 46.5   You Are Doran Dropout

Imagine that YOU are Doran Dropout. You do as little work as you can all though elementary and middle school. You drop out of high school as soon as you can get away with it.

Will it be easy for you to get a good job? Why not?

How will you feel when you can't get a good job, a job that you like and that pays well? Will you be happy about your job?

Will it be easy for you to have a nice life with a nice income? Why not?

Why is education (and training after high school) important?

Does education (and training) when you are young AFFECT YOUR WHOLE LIFE?

Are you going to graduate from high school?

Are you going on to a technical school or college?

Scenario 46.6   LaTesha Is a Leader

LaTesha likes to figure things out—and get things done. If the teacher asks, "Who would like to work on the school's recycling program?", LaTesha volunteers. "I don't know anything about it," thinks LaTesha, "but I can ask how to do it, and I can help figure it out." If her mother says, "What should we do for your brother's birthday?", LaTesha says, "Let's sit down and figure it out. I bet we can think of some good ideas!" LaTesha's attitude is always, *"I bet we can do it if we try!"*

Are people like LaTesha good to have around? Why?

Should we all try to figure things out and to get jobs done? Is that a good idea?

Does LaTesha have a good attitude: "WE CAN DO IT IF WE TRY!"?

Does that attitude help us get things done?

Should we all have that attitude?

Scenario 46.7   **Pat Ignores Safety Rules**

Pat ignores all safety rules. Walks across busy streets against the lights. Jaywalks downtown. Slides down banisters with splinters in them. Runs down all the stairs. Ignores fire drill bells. Sticks fingers into strange machines. Likes to play with broken glass. Teases strange dogs. Plays with dad's guns when nobody is home. Steals batteries out of smoke alarms. Plays tightrope walker on tall fences. Never buckles the seat belt.

If you were Pat, would you expect to have lots of injuries?

If you were Pat, would you expect to live long?

If you were Pat's friends, what would you think of Pat's habits?

Why are safety rules important?

Is the purpose of safety rules to protect us? Or do safety rules just get in the way of having fun?

Visualization:

"You Are the School Superintendent"

Objectives

Strengthening empathy for persons who do and do not value education, and person who do and do not adopt productive school and work habits.

Time Required

Introductions and narrations require about 10 minutes. Follow-up discussion of perceptions and feelings may require another 5 to 10 minutes.

Getting Started

Remind children of the importance of understanding other people's thoughts, feelings, and points of view. Mention that WE will be less likely to make big mistakes if we think about what happens to others when they have made mistakes with their values and their lives.

Have everyone "Get comfortable, shut your eyes, and imagine what is happening. Be sure to try to understand the thoughts and feelings of the people in the story." Read or paraphrase the scenarios fairly slowly, with pauses where indicated by ellipses (. . .).

Follow-Up

Each scenario includes its own follow-up questions. Help clarify the feelings and perceptions so that all students understand the harmful or productive behavior from the points of the view of the persons involved.

Try to elicit commitment to the idea that "This behavior (activity, value) is harmful to us because it hurts ourselves and our future lives."

A problem solving approach can be a good follow-up: "What is the problem here?" and "How can (should) we solve it?"

Visualization: Valuing Education, School and Work Habits

PROMPTNESS, WASTING OTHER PEOPLE'S TIME

Scenario 47.1 **You Are the School Superintendent**

Imagine that you are the superintendent of this entire school district . . . Lately you have been very, very busy with lots of problems . . . Your schools are too crowded . . . You don't have enough school buses . . . You don't have enough money for new computers . . . You have been helping to plan some new school learning activities . . . You have been interviewing new teachers and counselors who want jobs . . . You have been talking with the State Education Department about money for new classrooms, new computers, more buses, more books, and more videos for your schools . . . You are a VERY busy person.

Today you agreed to talk with some parents about organizing new soccer teams . . . Five parents had an appointment at 9:00 a.m., and now it is 10 minutes after nine o'clock . . . You wish you could work on your other projects, but you have to wait . . . At 9:15 three parents show up, and you talk about the weather while you all continue to wait . . . At 9:25 the other two parents walk in . . . They are laughing about the funny waitress in the coffee shop they just came from . . . You ask for a copy of their plan for the soccer teams . . . Mr. Fred Forgetful says, "Oh, gee whiz. I forgot. It's in the car . . . I'll have to go get it—can you wait just a minute" . . . He is gone for another five minutes . . . You and the parents talk some more about the weather . . . It's been cool and cloudy . . . But it might rain on Tuesday . . .

You finally get the report. . . . You look at the five parents and start to say, "Well now, this . . ." and then there is a knock on your door. . . . Your secretary says, "Mr. and Mrs. Thomas from Thomas Industries are here to see you about donating money to the school . . . They have an appointment and they are on time. Can you see them now?" . . .

How do you feel about the parents who were so late? Were they considerate and thoughtful?

Did they think about your point of view? Did they think about your problems? Did they think about your feelings?

It is important to be on time?

Is it fair to waste other people's time?

VALUING EDUCATION, ACHIEVEMENT MOTIVATION

Scenario 47.2   **You Are Lynn Jacobson, High School Drop Out**

Imagine you are seventeen years old . . . Your name is Lynn Jacobson . . . You dropped out of school a year ago . . . You have nothing to do . . . You have no job and no money . . . You are not very happy . . . Today you walk into the State Employment Office to see if they can find you a job . . . You have been here eleven times before . . . After waiting for an hour, you sit down at the desk of Ms. Wilson, a very nice woman who will try to help you . . .

Ms. Wilson says, "Good morning, Lynn. Have you had any luck finding a job?" . . . You say, "No" . . . She asks "Do you have any special skills or job training?" . . . You say, "No" . . . Ms. Wilson says, "I need nurses . . . I need dental assistants . . . I need people to operate computers . . . I need welders, carpenters, truck drivers, and salespeople . . . I need secretaries who can type and file . . . Why can't you do any of these things?" . . . You say, "Because I quit school . . . My friends told me that school was for suckers . . . They said that if I was *really* smart, I'd drop out of school . . . And now I can't get into a trade school or technical college without a high school diploma . . . I thought I knew what I was doing . . . I thought I was being smart" . . .

Ms. Wilson says, "I know you are capable of learning some valuable skills, Lynn . . . And I know you would like to be a trained, valuable person who could easily get a good job . . . It's too bad you did not stay in school . . . I'll see you next month, goodbye" . . .

Would you like to be Lynn, the person in this story?

Is it easy for Lynn to find a good job, a job that Lynn can be proud of? A job that pays well?

Was Lynn really smart to drop out of school? Why not?

Would you rather be an educated, trained person who can easily get a good job? Or someone like Lynn?

Is education important? How many reasons can you think of why education and training are important? (Job, pride, respect, money, security, . . .)

ACHIEVEMENT MOTIVATION, SELF-MOTIVATION

Scenario 47.3. **Thinking About Our Future: You Are Robbie Rabbit (For younger children)**

Imagine you are a young teenage rabbit named Robbie . . . You are just starting high school . . . You haven't thought much about your future . . . You haven't thought about what kind of adult, grown-up rabbit you would like to be . . . One day you are talking to the school guidance counselor, Mrs. Hare . . . You are talking about your future . . . Mrs. Hare is friendly and wants to help you think about your goals in life . . . She wants to help you work toward your goals . . . She asks, "What would you like to do when you graduate, Robbie? . . . What would you like to become? . . . How would you like to see yourself in a few years?" . . .

You wiggle your nose and fidget with your lucky foot . . . "Gee, I dunno'," you say . . . "Anything, I guess . . . Maybe it depends on if I'm lucky or not . . . What can I do about it?" . . . Mrs. Hare says, "You need some goals to work toward, Robbie . . . And you need to believe in yourself . . . You need to believe you can reach those goals . . . You need to take charge of your future . . . It takes more than just luck to become somebody you like and respect" . . .

You say, "But I'm just a young bunny . . . Getting a job or going to Cottontail College are still a long way off" . . . Mrs. Hare says, "We need to think about where we want to be in a year . . . in five years . . . in ten years . . . We need to make plans that will get us where we want to be . . . You should think about your future right now, Robbie . . . What kind of a grown up rabbit would you like to be? . . . Do you want to be proud of yourself? . . . Would you like to be a good computer operator? . . . Would you like to be a fine office worker or manager in the J. C. Bunny Store? . . . A good truck driver for the Cabbage Express Company? . . . A skillful welder or carpenter for High Hutch Construction Company? . . . A salesperson for Rabbit World Insurance? . . . Would you like to open your own Lettuce and Carrot Pizza Parlor? . . . Or would you like to become a nurse or a doctor at Hopping Hare Hospital? . . . An architect who designs ten-story tunnels? . . . Maybe an engineer? . . . A school teacher? . . . An accountant . . . Maybe a dentist? . . . There's lots of big front teeth to fix! . . .

"We need to think about our goals . . . We need to plan and to work toward those goals . . . And most of all, we need to believe in ourselves . . . We need to believe we can reach those goals" . . .

"You're right, Mrs. Hare . . . I don't want to be a dumb bunny without a good education and good training . . . I want to be ready for a good job or a career that I can be proud of . . . I want to look in the mirror and see a respectable rabbit—some bunny that I like!" . . .

> Which is best, to think about our goals in life and work toward them? Or just hope that we are lucky?
>
> Should we just depend on luck to help us become what we want to become?
>
> Can we control our lives? Or do we have to get tossed around in life, like a sock in a washing machine?
>
> What does this statement mean: "The harder I work, the luckier I get"?
>
> What does this statement mean: "You make your own luck"?
>
> (Both statements mean the same thing—If you want a successful life, you have to "Go for it!" You have to work for it.)

USING TIME WISELY (HUMOROUS, MORE OR LESS)

Scenario 47.3.   You Are Jamie, the Time Waster

> Imagine that you are Jamie . . . You have a bad habit of wasting time and putting things off . . . You never do homework on time . . . You don't make good use of class time . . . One day you are sitting in your seat looking at some new stickers from the gift shop . . . Your teacher, Mr. Frederickson, is at the front of the room . . . He says, "You have 20 minutes to read about Abraham Lincoln and be ready to answer some questions" . . . Mr. Frederickson looks directly at you . . . But you just keep looking at your stickers . . . You put them in different orders . . . Animals here, designs there . . . Then you arrange them by size, the biggest one down to the littlest one . . . You read the little print that says "Made in Taiwan, ROC" . . . Mr. Frederickson says, "You have just 10 minutes more" . . .

You wander to the pencil sharpener . . . Then you stroll back to your seat . . . You pick up the book and then start wondering, "What does ROC mean? . . . Rotten Old Cabbage? . . . Rutabaga, Onions, and Candy?" . . . "Time's up," announces Mr. Frederickson . . . "Jamie, let's hear your answers first! . . . What was Abraham Lincoln's nickname?" . . .

Well, Jamie, are you making good use of class time? What *should* you be doing in this story?

When should you, Jamie, play with your sticker collection?

If you were Mr. Frederickson, what would you think of Jamie's work habits?

Is Jamie being responsible?

Is Jamie doing a good job in school?

Is it important to make good use of our time? Why?

Questions and Discussion About Education and School and Work Habits

Objectives

To increase awareness, understanding, and commitment regarding valuing education, achievement motivation, and school and work habits.

Time Required

A few minutes (or seconds) may adequately cover a discussion. Ten minutes or more might be spent on interrelated questions.

More time would be needed if a teacher or parent follows up with a spontaneous brainstorming or "What would happen if . . . ?" problem.

Getting Started

Orient students to the purpose of the discussion. For example, "We're going to think about how important it is to get a good education and professional training when we are young adults. It will affect our entire lives."

Discussion Questions: Valuing Education, School and Work Habits

VALUING EDUCATION, ACHIEVEMENT MOTIVATION

48.1   What happens if we graduate from high school and we haven't bothered to develop our skills and talents as much as we might have? Maybe we can't read well, can't do math well, can't operate a microcomputer, and we can't write a letter or a simple report. Will it be easy to get a good job? Will it be easy to get into a good technical school or college? Will our lives be affected? Could we be unhappy and frustrated?

48.2   Is it important to develop our talents and skills? Why? (Jobs, pride, respect, money, security, fun, . . .)

48.3   How can we develop our skills and talents while we are young?

48.4   Does everyone have the same abilities? Same skills?

48.5   Even if someone is not the smartest or most talented person in the school, should they still try develop their skills and talents as much as possible?

48.6   Is effort—working hard—related to success in school and success in life? How?

48.7   Do we have control over whether we are successful in school and in life? How? (Effort, setting goals, working toward them, . . .)

48.8   Some people think success is just a matter of luck—they think they have nothing to do with developing their skills and getting a good job. Are they right? Is getting a good job and being successful in life just luck? Are you a sock just getting tossed around in the "Laundromat of Life"? Why not?

48.9   What does this statement mean?: "The harder I work, the luckier I get."

48.10   What does this statement mean?: "We make our own luck." (Statements 48.9 and 48.10 mean the same thing. If we want something, we have to "Go for it!" We have to work for it.)

48.11   Are we more likely to get something if we work for it?

48.12   What are goals?

48.13.   Should we think about our goals in life?

48.14   What are some worthwhile life goals? What do we want out of life? (Job success, happiness, good relationships with others, respect and dignity, to be thought of as "good persons," . . .)

48.15   What happens if we do NOT think about important goals and work toward them? Are we *more* likely or *less* likely to reach those goals?

48.16   What is the purpose of school? (To help you understand your world, develop your skills, become capable and talented adults who contribute to society, and help you be successful, reach your goals, and get more out of life. Others? . . .)

SCHOOL AND WORK HABITS

48.17   What happens when we do not pay attention in class?

48.18   Is it a good idea to pay attention to directions? Why?

48.19   What is *promptness*?

48.20   Do we like to be kept waiting?

48.21   What would your dentist think if you said, "Gee whiz, I'm sorry I'm a half-hour late; I was putting away my socks"? Is this fair to the dentist? Is this fair to the other people waiting for the dentist?

48.22   Is it a good idea to be prompt when people are waiting for you?

48.23   What is wasting time?

48.24   Are their times when it's all right to waste time? When?

48.25   Are their times when wasting time is not a good idea? When?

48.26   What does "using time wisely (well)" mean?

48.27   Why is "using time wisely (well)" a good idea?

48.28   Are there times when we should work hard and make good use of our time? And other times when we can relax, fool around, and waste time? Explain.

48.29   When you are working on a project, is it a good idea to complete the project? Or is it all right to just give up whenever you feel like it? Explain.

SAFETY RULES

48.30   What is "safety"? Is safety a good idea? Why?

48.31   Are people ever blinded, paralyzed, or badly injured because they didn't follow safely rules?

48.32   What are some safety rules? (Using seat belts, obeying traffic lights, looking both ways before crossing streets, following fire/tornado rules, not running down halls and stairs, not playing with broken glass or other sharp objects, not allowing young children to get into matches, poisons, or sharp or dangerous objects, . . . Drugs, guns, and drunk driving may be added . . .)

48.33   Are we likely to stay healthier and live longer if we pay attention to safety rules? Or are safety rules just for sissies and idiots?

Word Search and Crossword Puzzles:

Valuing Education, School and Work Habits

Again, two word search puzzles and one crossword puzzle. The puzzles use words and concepts related to valuing education, achievement motivation, and school and work habits. The puzzles are on separate pages so you may copy and use them without having children write in the book. Solutions are at the end of the chapter.

Word Search: About Education and GOOD Work Habits

In this puzzle you can search for words about education. There also are words related to good work habits. These habits will help you in school—and in life.

The words are printed left to right or top to bottom. One short word is printed from right to left (backwards).

Find these words and draw a ring around them.

Education	Graduate	Safety Rules	Use Time Well
Listen	Be Prompt	Try Hard	Goals
Neat Work	Plan		

```
U Z X C V R N N A L P
S A F E T Y R U L E S
E D U C A T I O N O B
T R T Y G R U I E P E
I A G Q R Y Y Z A S P
M I O M A H D L T O R
E J A P D A Z U W X O
W B L T U R S T O S M
E L S T A D A K R G P
L F I Z T M W Z K J T
L I S T E N X M Q W E
```

From *Teaching Values* published by Westwood Publishing Co. © 1996 Gary A. Davis

Word Search: About Ideas and Habits That Can Hurt YOU

In this puzzle you can search for words related to BAD working habits. These habits can hurt you in school—and in life.

All words are printed left to right or top to bottom.

Find these words and draw a ring around them.

Be Late	Waste Time	Excuses
Don't Try	Don't Listen	Break Rules
Drop Out	Sloppy Work	Waste Talent

```
W  A  S  T  E  T  I  M  E  D
A  W  L  Y  Z  R  T  X  B  O
S  D  O  N  T  T  R  Y  R  N
T  Q  P  U  D  E  B  R  E  T
E  T  P  Y  R  U  E  I  A  L
T  O  Y  P  O  Z  L  X  K  I
A  C  W  V  P  B  A  N  R  S
L  M  O  A  O  D  T  H  U  T
E  F  R  J  U  Z  E  X  L  E
N  K  K  W  T  S  Y  G  E  N
T  L  E  X  C  U  S  E  S  Z
```

Crossword Puzzle: Words About Education and Work Habits

Most words in this crossword puzzle are related to education and work habits—habits that can help you or hurt you. But a few words don't have much to do with anything.

Write the answers in the "checkerboard." Put one letter in each square. Start each answer in the square that has the same number as the question.

Write "Across" words in the regular way, from left to right.

Write "Down" words from top to bottom (vertically).

ACROSS

1. The BEST thing you can do for yourself is to "get a good _____."

6. We should not be late, we should be _____. (Rhymes with *tromped*.)

10. Albert's nickname.

11. We should always try to do a good _____.

13. People who ignore safety _____ can get hurt or killed.

14. We learn more, we get more done, and we do a better job if we use our _____ well.

15. Mohammed never hears instructions, because Mohammed never _____.

18. Abbreviation for "Standing Room Only." (This means the show is "sold out.")

19. Mohammed (in 15) should _____ attention.

From *Teaching Values* published by Westwood Publishing Co. © 1996 Gary A. Davis

DOWN

2. Someone who quits high school before graduating is a _____. (The answer is not "dummy." The answer rhymes with *cop out*.)

3. Nickname for a policeman or policewoman.

4. After high school, the BEST thing you can do for yourself is go ____ a technical school or a college.

5. Opposite of "off."

6. Opposite of "Ma."

7. We won't succeed at ANYTHING, unless we _____ hard.

8. JoAnne always says, "I didn't have time," "I had a headache," "I forgot," "My canary ate my book," "I had to go to my grandmother's." JoAnne makes _____. (Rhymes with *pecks mooses*.)

9. People who ignore _____ rules can get hurt or killed.

12. Afternoon is p.m., morning is _____.

15. If you work hard, try hard, you can WIN in life. If you don't even try, you are certain to _____.

16. Opposite of "Go."

17. In school, and on the job, it is important to do _____ work. (Rhymes with *feet*.)

Solutions to Puzzles in This Chapter

Word Search About Education and Good Working Habits

```
U                 N   A   L  P
 S A F E T Y  R I U   L   E  S
 E D U C   A   R   O   N      B
 T   A   G R I       E      E
 T I   C   R R       A      P
 M   G   R A   Y       T      R
 E   O   A H       W      O
 W   A   D A       O      M
 E   L   U R       R      P
 L   S   A D       K      T
 L       T
 L I S T E N
```

Word Search: About Ideas and Habits That Can HURT You

```
W A S T E T I M  E   D
A   S        R   Y  B  O
S D L O N T T T  R   E  N
T   O     D    B  A  T
E   P     R    E  K  L
T   P     O    L  R  I
A   Y     P    A  U  S
L   W     O    T  L  T
E   O     U    E  E  E
N   R     T       S  N
T   K E X C U S E S
```

Crossword Puzzle

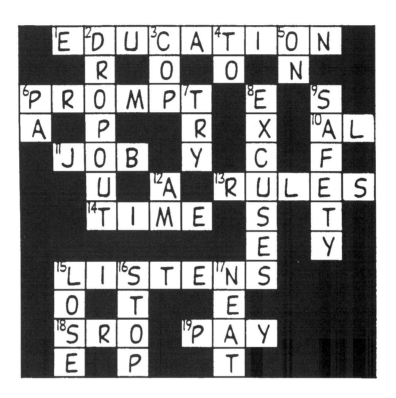

Part VIII

Energy and Environment

50

Energy and Environment:

"What Would Happen If . . . Everyone Left Messes?"

Energy and Environment Values

Quite properly, most people are becoming more environment and conservation conscious. Many schools, teachers, and parents foster environment- and conservation-mindedness with such strategies as:

Involving children in recycling programs at home and school.

School grounds, yard, and sometimes road clean-ups.

Reminding children to "Don't waste (electricity, heat, water, food, paper, pencils, supplies, money, . . .)."

Reminding children to "Don't make a mess," "Don't leave a mess," "Take care of your things," . . . .

Donating unwanted clothes and household items to "thrift stores."

Raising awareness of threatened natural resources and endangered species.

On a visit to Lucerne, Switzerland, a few years ago, I saw recycling bins located on the grounds of an elementary school. What an excellent strategy, I thought, to involve children in recycling and foster values related to conservation.

In this section, specific values pertaining to conserving energy and resources and respecting our environment will relate to:

Conserving natural resources, recycling

Not making/leaving messes; not littering

Conserving heat, electricity

Caring for one's own property

Caring for others' property

Conserving school materials

Objectives

In this chapter, each "What Would Happen If . . . ?" problem seeks to increase awareness, understanding, and commitment related to the environmental and conservation values described above. Some topics overlap with values discussed in earlier sections, for example, taking care of other people's property.

Time Required

Three to 10 minutes per activity, depending upon the problem and student interest, plus time for introductions and follow-ups.

Getting Started

Introduce the particular environmental or conservation value(s), perhaps by discussing the meaning of the focus topic (e.g., *conserving natural resources, littering, wasting supplies*, etc.). You might ask for definitions ("What do we mean by *conserving* or *littering*?") or examples ("Where do we see people *littering*?").

Explain that "We are going to think about what happens as a result of (e.g., wasting, littering)." Explain that "The problem will begin with 'What would happen if . . . ?' and you can use your imagination to think about what happens when people (waste energy, waste supplies, litter, recycle, . . .).

As always, try to elicit *commitments* to constructive values and behavior: "Is it a good idea to litter?" "Are you the kind of person who will toss junk out your car window?"

"What Would Happen If . . . ?" Problems

Problem 50.1 **What would happen if EVERYONE left messes in our streets, highways, and parks?** Everyone is a litterer. *Nobody respects the environment.* McDonald's wrappers and soda cans get tossed out the car window or dropped on the sidewalk. Everybody leaves messes in the parks and the zoo. What would happen?

Which kind of environment looks better, a clean one or one filled with mess and garbage?

Should we respect our environment? Should we try to keep it clean?

Are you the kind of person who will trash our environment?

Problem 50.2 **What would happen if everyone carefully cleaned up after their picnics in the park, and nobody ever tossed trash out their car windows?**

Would our parks and roads be cleaner and prettier?

Should we try to keep our environment clean and pretty for everyone? Or dirty and ugly?

Are you the kind of person who will trash our parks and roads?

Problem 50.3 **What would happen if everyone were really messy in our school?** Nobody uses trash cans. Everybody tosses things on the floor. Nobody cleans up after they finish working. Nobody cleans up after they spill things. What would happen?

Do we like a clean room? Clean halls? Clean school grounds? Or do we like a messy room? Messy halls? Messy school grounds?

Which is better, neat and clean? Or messy and dirty?

Should we try to keep our school environment clean?

Problem 50.4 **What would happen if everyone helped keep the school neat and clean?** We all put trash in trash cans. We all pick up papers and junk in the halls and school yard. We all clean up extra carefully after working on projects.

Do we like a clean school? Clean halls? Clean school grounds? Or do we like a messy school? Messy halls? Messy school grounds?

Which is better, neat and clean? Or messy and dirty?

Should we try to keep our school environment clean?

Problem 50.5 **What would happen if everyone in the school wasted as many school supplies as they possibly could?** We lose all of our pencils. We waste all of our paper supplies. We break up the chalk and toss it away. We tear our books and write all over them. What would happen?

Do school supplies cost a lot of money?

Is wasting supplies like wasting somebody's money?

Would we want our own things broken, torn up, and thrown away?

Is it right to waste the school's books and supplies?

Problem 50.6   **What would happen if we did not take care of other people's property?** If we use someone's book, pen, bicycle, cassette player, or maybe a pair of their gloves, we just let them get torn up, broken, rained on, or lost. What would happen?

Do we like people to take care of our things?

Do we like people to return our things in good condition?

Should we take care of other people's property?

Problem 50.7   **What happens if we take GOOD care of other people's property?** If we use someone's book, pen, bicycle, or cassette player, we return them in good condition. We don't let them get torn up, broken, rained on, or lost. What would happen?

Do we like people to take care of our things?

Do we like people to return our things in good condition?

Should we take care of other people's property?

Problem 50.8   **What would happen if nobody cared for their own property?** We bang up our bicycles. We break our expensive roller blades. We leave our cassette players out in the rain. We play softball and soccer in our best clothes. We leave things where they can get stolen. What would happen?

Do our toys, athletic equipment, and clothes last longer when we take care of them?

Is it a good idea to take care of our valuable things?

Problem 50.9   Paper is made from trees, isn't it. **What would happen if nobody recycled school paper, office paper, or newspapers, AND everyone wasted as much paper as they could?**

Is wasting paper the same as wasting trees?

Is recycling paper the same as saving trees?

Is saving trees a good idea? Do we like trees in our forests?

Paper costs money, doesn't it. Is wasting paper also wasting money?

Problem 50.10 **What would happen if everyone in the world wasted as much food as they possibly could?** One bite of anything, and into the trash can it goes! Fill up your tray in the cafeteria, and then dump it all into the trash.

Is wasting food like wasting money? Why? (It costs money to buy more.)

Is it fair to people who buy the food (parents, the school) for us to waste it?

Is it a good idea to waste food?

Should we just take what we can eat?

Problem 50.11 **What would happen if everyone wasted as much electricity as they could?** We leave all the lights on all the time. Everyone runs their home air conditioners from May to September. Maybe in winter everyone tries to heat their homes and apartments with the electric oven.

When we waste electricity, do we also waste money? Why is that?

Who has to pay for the electricity?

When we waste electricity, do we also waste coal (or water power from the dam)?

Problem 50.12 **What would happen if we all were very careful about conserving electricity?** We turn off lights. We try to use air conditioners and electric heaters as little as possible.

Would we save money for someone?

Would we conserve energy?

Would we be sharing responsibility for our natural resources (coal, water power)?

Should we all try to conserve electricity?

Problem 50.13 **What would happen if everyone in the world wasted as much gas and oil as they could?** We all turn our gas furnaces up to 80 degrees (instead of 68). We all buy cars and trucks that burn up lots of gas and oil. Nobody recycles their car oil. What could (will) happen?

When we waste gas and oil, do we also waste money?

Is it a good idea NOT to waste gas and oil?

Is it a good idea to recycle the old oil from cars and trucks?

Brainstorming and Reverse Brainstorming:

"How Can We Waste Electricity?"

Brainstorming and reverse brainstorming present many opportunities for exploring values related to energy and the environment. Children can think of many ways to conserve and protect, and many ways to waste and destroy.

Some problems are true creative challenges, for example, "How can we make electricity conserve (or waste) itself?" and "How can we raise community awareness of littering?" These kinds of problems typically take much longer than other brainstorming problems in this book. Class recycling projects or school/community awareness projects (for example, a puppet show, slide show, or shopping center posters that illustrate good energy/environment values) may develop from these kinds of brainstorming problems.

Objectives

To raise awareness, understanding, and commitment relating to energy and environment values.

Time Required

Approximately 5 to 15 minutes. Longer for problems that may result in class recycling projects or school/community awareness projects.

Getting Started

Be sure everyone understands the concepts and vocabulary. If needed, probe for and explain concept meanings: "What do we mean by *recycle, conserve,* and *respect the environment*?"

Explain that we are going to think about (a topic) by using brainstorming (or reverse brainstorming).

Review brainstorming rules: "We will think of all the ideas we can; we want a long list of ideas. We don't criticize each other's ideas."

With Reverse Brainstorming, remind children that "With Reverse Brainstorming, we turn the problem around. We think of how to make something WORSE. Reverse Brainstorming helps us understand a situation better.

Prod children for additional ideas: "Anyone else have an idea?" "Shonita, do you have an idea?"

Record ideas on the chalkboard or have a volunteer do so.

A teacher may use a large-group or small-group format. Small groups may work on the same problem or different problems. A spokesperson reports the group's ideas to the class.

Note that some problems are in pairs, for example, "How can we make a situation worse?" and "How can we make it better?"

Follow-Up

The following are some questions for stimulating discussion following a brainstorming or reverse brainstorming problem.

(With reverse brainstorming) Do we ever do this? (Answer: Yes, a lot!)

Is it a good idea to . . . (waste electricity, conserve heat, ruin library books, ruin other people's things, protect our things from damage or theft, trash our environment by littering, etc.)

Do thoughtful people do this?

Do people who are concerned about our environment do this?

Is the world a cleaner, nicer (messier, uglier) place when we do this?

Have people ever broken or damaged your things? How did you feel?

When people break your things, are they thinking about your feelings?

Do people have the right to damage your things?

Do you have the right to damage other people's things?

Should WE do this?

Are you the kind of people who will do this?

Brainstorming and Reverse Brainstorming Problems

[Reverse Brainstorming problems are marked with an "(R)."]

Problem 51.1	How many ways can you think of to waste electricity at home? You know, REALLY run up the light bill? (R)
Problem 51.2	How many ways can you think of to save electricity at home?
Problem 51.3	How many ways can you think of to waste electricity at school? (R)
Problem 51.4	How many plans or ways can you think of to conserve electricity at school?
Problem 51.5	How could we get the WHOLE CITY or the WHOLE STATE to conserve more electricity? Use you imagination?
Problem 51.6	How could we make electricity "save (conserve) itself"?
Problem 51.7	How could we make electricity "waste itself"? (R)
Problem 51.8	How could we make heat "conserve itself"?
Problem 51.9	How could we make heat "waste itself"? (R)
Problem 51.10	Imagine it is 200 years in the future. How will heat or electricity be saved?
Problem 51.11	How many different ways can we waste school supplies. How could we use up the whole year's supplies in one week? (R)
Problem 51.12	How many ways can we think of to conserve school supplies (to make sure that we have enough to last the year)?

Problem 51.13 How many ways can you think of to ruin our textbooks and library books? (R)

Problem 51.14 How many ways can you think of to protect textbooks and library books?

Problem 51.15 How many ways can you think of to ruin a new pair of jeans or a new jacket? (R)

Problem 51.16 How many ways can you think of to be a real careless person who loses things and lets things get ruined? (R)

Problem 51.17 How many ways can you think of to be very careful and protect your things from being lost or damaged?

Problem 51.18 How many ways can you think of to damage, destroy, or lose other people's things? (R)

Problem 51.19 How can we help our things to get stolen? (R)

Problem 51.20 How many ways can you think of to protect our things from being stolen?

Problem 51.21 Imagine you are 16 years old and you have a car. How many different kinds of junk can you think of to throw out your car window, so you can make our streets and highways look as ugly as possible? (R)

Problem 51.22 How can we raise community awareness of littering? How can we help others learn to stop littering?

Problem 51.23 Imagine a picnic in your favorite park. How can you leave the biggest mess imaginable? (R)

Problem 51.24 Imagine a picnic in your favorite park. How can you leave the park *cleaner* than when you found it?

Chapter

Analogical Thinking:

"How Is a Messy Person Like an Out-of-Tune Clarinet?"

Objectives

To use analogical thinking to help children think about and make decisions and commitments regarding energy and our environment.

Time Required

Often just a minute or two, perhaps a few seconds. Be ready with additional analogy problems, a follow-up discussion to clarify the analogical connection, or another activity. However, try not to allow a thinking session to end too quickly; encourage children to "put on their thinking caps" and try to find more analogical connections.

Getting Started

Remind children of the meaning of "analogical thinking": It's thinking about how things are alike. Also, be sure children understand the conservation and environmental concepts to be discussed

Explain that "We are going use analogies to help us think about (conserving energy, protecting our environment, taking care of other people's things, taking care of our own things, etc.)." Encourage children to think of as many comparisons as they can. If a child contributes an unclear idea, explain the analogical connection yourself or have the child do so.

Record ideas on the chalkboard. In the classroom, a small-group format can be used. Children would be given two or three minutes (or more) to think of one or more analogies, which are then reported to the class. Groups may work on the same analogy problem or different ones.

Analogy Problems About Energy, Environment, Caring for Property

Problem 52.1	How is wasting electricity like piling up dollar bills and burning them?
Problem 52.2	How is a wasting electricity like wearing shoes that are too small? (We hurt ourselves. We don't have to do it. It doesn't make sense. It's not a good idea. It can get more and more painful . . .)
Problem 52.3	How is conserving electricity like putting money in the bank.
Problem 52.4	How is wasting heat in our homes or school like mailing our money to millionaires.
Problem 52.5	How is wasting natural resources (like oil, trees, and iron ore) like a picnic with 10 hot dogs for 50 people? (You are going to run out.)
Problem 52.6	How is wasting school supplies like writing with your left hand (or right hand, for lefties)? (It's making things hard for yourself. It's unnecessary . . .)
Problem 52.7	How is wasting school supplies and ruining our school books like sticking your finger in the pencil sharpener.
Problem 52.8	How is being careful with school supplies (conserving school supplies) like putting money in the bank?
Problem 52.9	How is wasting food at home like breaking your own toys? (It costs money to replace them both? It's not logical or smart. You need them both . . .)
Problem 52.10	How is caring for other people's property like being a great detective? (You are being smart; using your intelligence. You are being careful. You are helping others. You are being logical . . .)

Problem 52.11 How is damaging other people's property like stomping on someone's foot?

Problem 52.12 How is protecting other people's property like being a thoughtful, nice person?

Problem 52.13 How is a messy person like an out-of-tune clarinet?

Problem 52.14 How is someone who litters like a computer that doesn't work? (It can't think. It's not logical. It doesn't do what it's supposed to do. It's useless. It makes things difficult for us. It looks smart, but isn't . . .)

Problem 52.15 How is someone who cares about a clean environment like a nice butterfly? (They make the world prettier. They like a good environment. They are sensitive to pollution and messes . . .)

Chapter

53

Visualization and Taking Other Perspectives:

"Imagine You Are Willy Wasteful"

Objectives

To use empathy to increase children's understanding and commitment related to wasting versus conserving, respecting versus disrespecting our environment.

To raise awareness of taking care of one's own and others' property.

Time Required

Introductions and narrations require 5 to 10 minutes. Follow-up discussion of perceptions and feelings may require another 5 to 10 minutes.

Getting Started

Remind children of the importance of *empathy*—of trying to see things from someone else's point of view, putting yourself in their shoes, and understanding their thoughts and feelings.

Have everyone "Get comfortable, shut your eyes, and imagine what is happening. Try hard to understand the thoughts and feelings of the people in the story." Read or paraphrase the scenarios fairly slowly, with pauses where indicated by ellipses (. . .).

Follow-Up

Each scenario includes its own follow-up questions. Be sure to clarify the feelings and perceptions so that all students understand the problem (or the positive behavior) from the point of the view of persons involved.

A problem solving approach is especially suitable as a follow-up activity for these scenarios—because each one presents a fairly clear "problem." Remember our simple problem solving approach? (1) "What is the problem?" (2) "How can (or should) we solve it?"

Visualization and Taking Other Perspectives

Scenario 53.1. **You Are Willy Wasteful**

Imagine that you are "Willy Wasteful" and you are in school today . . . You notice that your pencil is a little dull, and so you drop it the trash can and get a nice new sharp one . . . At art time, you accidentally make a small mark on a large sheet of expensive drawing paper . . . So you crumple it up, toss it away, and get another . . . Yesterday you spilled some glue on a stack of new computer disks . . . They went into the trash, too . . . Last week you were looking out the window while you carried the aquarium . . . You dropped it and smashed it . . . You always scribble and draw cartoon pictures in new books . . . And you like to tear a few pages . . . Your teacher is Ms. Cortez . . . Ms. Cortez will have to buy more pencils, drawing paper, computer disks, and a new aquarium with her own money to make up for your wastefulness . . .

> Well, Willy Wasteful, is it right for you to waste school supplies and break equipment? Why not?
>
> How would YOU feel if you had to buy pencils, drawing paper, computer disks, and new aquarium out of your own money—because somebody else threw them away or ruined them? Would you be pleased?
>
> Does it make sense to waste supplies and ruin or break things at school?
>
> *Should we be careful with school supplies and other things at school?*

Scenario 53.2. **You Are a Homeowner**

Imagine you are all grown up. . . . You saved up your money, you went house-hunting for six months, and just last week you bought a nice new home . . . But every morning, in front of your new home and all along the street, you find soda cans . . . beer cans . . . cheeseburger wrappers . . . some newspaper pages . . . sometimes a diaper . . . and sometimes other junk that people don't want, and have tossed in front of your home . . . This garbage makes your yard and street look awful . . . You wonder why people do this . . . Don't they know better? . . . Don't they respect your rights? . . .

How do you feel about this garbage?

Why do you think people toss garbage out of their car windows?

What do we think of people who do this?

Do thoughtful people litter the streets and highways?

Are you going to be a litterer?

Are you going to mess up people's front yards?

Are you going to mess up streets and highways?

Scenario 53.3   **You are Marty Messalot—World Champion Messy Person**

Imagine that your name is Marty Messalot . . . You are a very sloppy, careless person . . . At home, your bedroom looks like it was bombed . . . You mother put a sign on your door that says "Disaster Area—Enter at Your Own Risk!" . . . Clothes are dangling out of open drawers . . . Dirty socks and shirts are all over the floor, mixed in with some clean ones . . . One sock is hanging from the lamp . . . Under the socks and shirts are books and magazines and some old toys and games . . . Sometimes you have to step on the magazines to get through the room . . . Torn pages are everywhere . . . Most of the old toys have been stepped on and broken . . . All of the boxes for your games are crushed . . . Some boxes are open and the pieces scattered . . . You think to yourself, "Those games aren't much good any more, but I'll keep them anyway." . . . At breakfast you spill milk and juice . . . You leave toast crumbs and bits of strawberry jam all over the table . . .

At school you keep cramming more and more things into your locker . . . There's stacks of math and English work sheets from last year . . . a broken yard stick . . . three dead batteries and some pens that won't write . . . a burned out light bulb . . . one glove . . . You think the other one is home with the socks and shirts . . . And there is the frisbee you borrowed a month ago . . . You wish its owner would come and get it . . . You'd like to find your new pen that is in there somewhere . . . But you look at the mess and just close the door . . .

Today your report on the moon is due . . . The report is wrinkled because you sat on it on the bus . . . There is a little strawberry jam on page 2 . . . It's still sticky . . . There are some big black smudges where you started to erase, then changed your mind . . . The back side of the report has a black gritty footprint on it . . . It slipped under your foot while you were at your locker . . . After you get a book from the bookshelf, the shelf is messed up from one end to the other . . . Your teacher, Mr. Washington, reminds you to "Please try to be neater" . . . But somehow you don't really understand the meaning of the word "neat" . . .

Which is better, neat or messy? Why?

Should we take care of our books, magazines, toys, games, and other things? Why?

Is it necessary to be as messy as Marty Messalot?

Is it fair to make messes for others to look at? To clean up?

Should we make an effort to be neat? To do neat work?

Scenario 53.4.   Larry Loaner

Larry Loaner is a very nice person . . . He likes to do favors for people . . . His friends often borrow things from him . . . Last week Larry loaned his new cassette player to Terrell . . . When Terrell returned it, the flip-up door was broken . . . Larry also loaned Terrell his best cassettes—classic Beatles music! . . . One tape was returned with peanut butter on it . . . Another was all tangled up . . . He loaned a book to Jennifer . . . When Jennifer returned it, she had written telephone messages all over it . . . At school he loaned two pens, one to Jackie and one to Leon . . . They didn't bother to return them at all . . . Larry wonders if trying to help people is such a good idea . . .

Do you like things to be returned broken or messed up? Is it fair?

Should we take care of other people's property?

Scenario 53.5.   Conserving electricity, heat

Imagine you are all grown up . . . You live in your own home . . . YOU have to pay your own electric bill and your own heating bill . . . But you don't worry about it . . . When it's cold, you keep the heat turned up high and you don't bother to close the windows . . . You might run an electric heater or two also, because you like the house nice and warm . . . You let hot water run down the drain while you talk on the phone for half an hour . . . You always leave all the lights on—it's such a bother to flip those little switches . . . Your basement and porch lights are on all day and all night. . . . When you leave in the morning, you leave the lights on . . . and the radio . . . and maybe the TV . . . In the spring, summer, and fall you run your air conditioner full blast day and night, all the time . . . If the house gets too cold, you just open some windows and doors . . . Every month you get your electric bill in the mail . . . And your heating bill . . . the bills are HUGE . . . You think to yourself, "That darn electric company!" . . . "And that darn gas company . . . They just charge too much for electricity and gas!"

Why are your electricity and gas bills so large?

Should you keep the heat turned up high?

Should you wear a sweater in the house and turn the heat down?

Should you leave lights on all day and all night?

Should your windows be open while the heat is turned up?

Should you let the hot water run in the sink when you are on the phone?

Should you run your air conditioner all the time in the spring, summer, and fall?

Should we leave lights on when nobody is in the room?

Should we keep the heat turned up really high?

Should we waste hot water?

How else can we conserve electricity and heat in our homes?

How can we conserve electricity and heat in the school?

Should we think about saving electricity and heat?

Scenario 53.6. Littering

Imagine you are a jogger . . . you just love to go jogging around the park . . . Today you are out jogging . . . You look at the trees in the park . . . There are flower gardens with tulips and roses . . . Some robins are chirping . . . Children are swinging on the swings and sliding down the slippery slide . . . Then a car filled with teenagers passes by, and they toss out a boxful of empty beer bottles . . . The box hits the ground and the beer bottles scatter all over . . . Most of them break . . . Then you notice that lots of soda cans, beer cans, and burger wrappers have been dumped around the park . . . You wonder why these thoughtless people make messes that others must clean up . . . YOU can see that it makes the park ugly . . . YOU understand that somebody will have to clean up their garbage . . . Why can't THEY understand these things? . . . They're not being intelligent or fair . . .

Then you see some picnickers pack up their ice chest, their picnic basket, and their blanket . . . They climb into their car and drive away . . . But they left some dirty paper plates, a pork and beans can, some napkins, and a potato chip bag . . . Their mess is ugly too . . . And you know that someone will have to clean up after them also . . .

Are parks and roadways prettier or uglier when people throw their trash all over the place?

What kind of people mess up roads and parks with beer cans and burger wrappers? Are they considerate? Thoughtful? Intelligent?

Do they think about other people's rights and feelings?

Is it fair to leave messes for others to clean up?

Are you the type of person who will mess up parks and streets with your trash?

Will you make parks and streets ugly with your trash?

Will you make messes that somebody else has to clean up?

54

Questions and Discussion About Energy and the Environment

Objectives

To increase awareness, understanding, and commitment regarding energy and environment issues, including taking care of our own and others' property.

Time Required

A few minutes (or seconds) may adequately cover a discussion. Ten minutes might be spent on interrelated questions. More time would be needed if a parent or teacher follows up with a spontaneous brain-storming or "What would happen if . . . ?" problem, or a problem solving approach ("What is the problem?" and "How can we solve it?").

Getting Started

Orient students to the purpose and topic of the discussion. For example, "We're going to think about our environment—and keeping it clean and attractive."

Discussion Questions About Energy, Environment, Caring for Our Own and Others' Property

CONSERVING ENERGY

54.1 Why is it important to conserve electricity?

54.2 Why is it important to conserve heat?

54.3 If you were paying the bills, what would you think of people in your home or your school who were wasting lots of electricity and heat? Are they thoughtful? Considerate? Concerned about wasting money? Concerned about wasting natural resources (coal, gas)?

WASTING SUPPLIES

54.4 Let's think about school materials—pencils, paper, work sheets, work books, computer disks, and so on. Should we waste our supplies as FAST as we can? Why not?

54.5 What do we think of people who waste school materials? Are they behaving intelligently? Are they being fair to others? Are they being fair to the school, which must pay for the materials?

TAKING CARE OF OUR OWN AND OTHERS' PROPERTY

54.6 Imagine that YOU are your parents. You just bought your 10-year old child a $35 Walkman headset. A week later your dear little child tells you, "Gee Whiz, I left it somewhere, but I can't remember where!" What do you think about this?

54.7 Should we care for our property? Or is it all right to leave things lying around where they can get lost, stolen, or broken?

54.8 Have you ever loaned things and had them returned broken or torn? Were you happy about that? How did you feel?

54.9 What do you think of people who damage other people's property? Are they being fair? Responsible? Trustworthy?

54.10 What should you do if you accidentally damage something that belongs to someone else? What would be fair?

MAKING MESSES

54.11   Is it all right to do messy school work? Is this a good habit? Why not?

54.12   How do you feel when somebody leaves a mess for you to clean up? Is this fair? Do you like that person a lot more? Do you respect that person more?

54.13   Is it all right to make messes at home for somebody else to clean up?

54.14   Do you want to think of yourself as a messy person? Why not?

LITTERING

54.15   Have you seen highways and parks littered with garbage? What do you thing about that? Are parks and roadways prettier when they are covered with trash?

54.16   Have you seen people throw stuff out of their car windows? Is this intelligent, thoughtful behavior?

54.17   What do we think of people who leave garbage in public places, or who throw trash out their car windows? Are they really fine, wonderful people? Is this intelligent, thoughtful behavior? Do they have a right to do this? *Should we leave garbage in parks and along our highways?*

Word Search and Crossword Puzzles:

Energy and Our Environment

The following pages contain our final two word search puzzles and one crossword puzzle. The puzzles use words and concepts related to energy and environment issues, as well as taking care of our own and others' property. The puzzles are on separate pages so you may copy and use them without having children write in the book. Solutions are at the end of the chapter.

Word Search for GOOD Words About Energy and Our Environment

This word search puzzle has "good" words related to conserving energy and keeping our environment clean and pretty.

The words are printed left to right or top to bottom. One word is printed from right to left (backwards).

Find these words and draw a ring around them.

Environment	Recycle	Save
Neat	Energy	Conserve
Take Care	Clean	

```
E  N  E  R  G  Y  C
N  R  Y  E  T  Q  O
V  T  Q  C  A  F  N
I  Z  S  Y  K  L  S
R  K  W  C  E  X  E
O  J  C  L  C  D  R
N  C  L  E  A  N  V
M  Y  H  I  R  B  E
E  G  X  Z  E  U  W
N  E  A  T  V  M  A
T  C  E  V  A  S  R
```

From *Teaching Values* published by Westwood Publishing Co. © 1996 Gary A. Davis

Word Search for Not-So-Good Words About Energy and Our Environment

This is a word search puzzle about "not-so-good" words related to conserving energy and keeping our environment clean and beautiful.

The words are printed left to right or top to bottom. One word is printed from right to left (backwards).

Find these words and draw a ring around them.

Dirty	Leave Mess	Careless
Don't Care	Don't Recycle	Waste
Trash	Litter	

```
D  B  D  X  Y  L  I  X
O  W  O  F  U  E  O  J
N  Y  N  T  R  A  S  H
T  N  T  C  T  V  D  T
R  Z  C  M  V  E  P  W
E  W  A  X  S  M  Y  A
C  A  R  E  L  E  S  S
Y  K  E  Q  D  S  R  T
C  N  R  G  L  S  H  E
L  I  T  T  E  R  Z  M
E  W  L  Y  T  R  I  D
```

Crossword Puzzle About Saving Energy and Respecting Our Environment

Most words in this crossword puzzle are related to protecting our environment, keeping it clean, and saving energy. But a few words don't have much to do with anything.

Write the answers in the "checkerboard." Put one letter in each square. Start each answer in the square that has the same number as the question.

Write "Across" words in the regular way, from left to right.

Write "Down" words from top to bottom (vertically).

ACROSS

1. The two main words for this puzzle are environment and _____.

4. Should we waste energy and mess up our environment?

5. Some people leave their _____ in parks and picnic areas. (Rhymes with *far bridge*.)

6. Initials of the news company called the Associated Press.

8. We can save natural resources if we _____ our aluminum cans, glass bottles, plastic milk jugs, and other things.

11. Theodore Roosevelt's initials.

12. We should not drop our garbage on the floor, we should _____ it in the trash can.

14. We should not leave _____ in parks, at home, or in school. (Rhymes with *presses*.)

From *Teaching Values* published by Westwood Publishing Co. © 1996 Gary A. Davis

15. Nobody has the right to _____ our parks and roads. (Rhymes with *twitter*.)

16. Litter does not make parks, roads, and school grounds beautiful, it makes them _____.

DOWN

1. The two main words for this puzzle are _____ and energy.

2. Abbreviation for England.

3. People who mess up our environment just don't _____. (Rhymes with *bear*.)

4. Some people are messy, some people are _____. (Rhymes with *feet*.)

7. We should take care of our own property, and we should take care of others' _____.

9. It's a good idea for everyone to help _____ our natural resources, like gas, oil, coal, and lumber.

10. Our environment will be prettier if we are not _____ with our trash. (Rhymes with *bear-less*.)

13. A rodent that is bigger than a mouse, and lives in back alleys and garbage dumps.

16. Opposite of down.

17. Louise's nickname.

Solutions to Puzzles

Word Search for GOOD Words About Energy and Our Environment

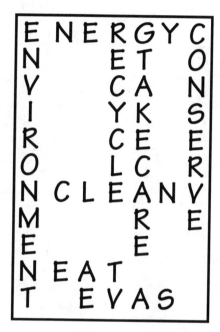

Word Search for Not-So-Good Words About Energy and Our Environment

Crossword Puzzle

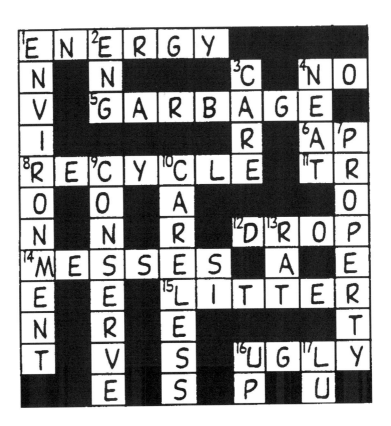

56

Final Examination:

Values and Your Dreams

Let's think about decisions and choices that can help you reach YOUR dreams.

Let's think about things that will HELP or HURT your chances for a good future life.

> You just have to use common sense.
> Just think a little bit.
> It won't hurt.

Think about "good values" and "bad values."

Ask yourself these questions:

> Does this hurt other people?
> Does it hurt me?
> Can it hurt my life?
> Would my mother, grandmother, or teacher do this?
> If I do this, would my family, my friends, and other people lose respect for me?

As you read each statement, also ask yourself:

Will this activity probably HELP my chances for a good future life?
(Will this ACTION have GOOD CONSEQUENCES?)

Or will it HURT my chance for a GOOD future life—for the YEARS
and YEARS and YEARS that I will be an adult.
(Will this ACTION have BAD CONSEQUENCES?)

	Will HELP My Life	Will HURT My Life
1. Jake drives a big Cadillac. He got the money by selling drugs. I would like to be like Jake.	_____	_____
2. It would be just fine to get caught selling drugs and go to prison for a few years.	_____	_____
3. I will try to develop ALL the skills and abilities I can—in reading, writing, math, science, computers, and music. And in swimming, basketball, and other sports, too.	_____	_____
4. I don't care about my health. The important thing is to have fun.	_____	_____
5. The TV cartoon boy Bart Simpson doesn't work hard in school. He is "Proud to be an Underachiever." I should be like Bart Simpson.	_____	_____

	Will HELP My Life	Will HURT My Life
6. There is nothing wrong with a little stealing and burglary when I get bigger. I won't get caught. Besides, they don't do anything to kids.	_____	_____
7. I plan to work hard in school, then go on to technical school or college, then get a good job.	_____	_____
8. When I get a little older, I plan to carry a gun to school—then I'll be grown up and powerful! I'll get respect!	_____	_____
9. I want others to know that I am a good person, someone who is honest and trustworthy.	_____	_____
10. Smoking is really cool, even if it does cause cancer and heart problems.	_____	_____
11. It's a good idea to be a nasty, grouchy, sarcastic person—and maybe a bully too.	_____	_____
12. It's a good idea to be honest and fair with other people. It's just the right way to live. People will respect me more, too.	_____	_____
13. It's good to have empathy, to try to understand other people's feelings.	_____	_____

	Will HELP My Life	Will HURT My Life
14. It's okay to steal and destroy other people's property. In fact, it's fun.	_____	_____
15. Its best to respect other people's rights, to return their things, and not to damage their property. (Because that's how I want to be treated!)	_____	_____
16. It's good to think about my future life—and NOT make BIG mistakes that will trash it (like dropping out of school, or becoming a drug dealer or a criminal).	_____	_____
17. Friends and people who love you are valuable. You should treat them with honesty, fairness, and friendliness.	_____	_____
18. For girls, the most important thing in life is to try to be really, really sexy.	_____	_____
19. If my friends want me to have bad values—like being rude, taking drugs, and dropping out of school—I should do whatever my friends want me to.	_____	_____
20. If I develop abilities and skills, I can get a good-paying job. I can buy nice things.	_____	_____

	Will HELP My Life	Will HURT My Life
21. It doesn't matter if I lie, cheat, steal, don't return things, and don't show up on time. Who cares if I am irresponsible.	_____	_____
22. I don't need to think about other people's rights to fair and pleasant treatment. That's their problem!	_____	_____

Answers: I hope you know all of the right answers. Your values and your future life depend on it.

"We all make decisions that affect the course of our lives." ...
"Your future is whatever you make it— so make it a good one!"
From the movie,
Back to the Future, Part III

Index